The Way to Freedom

The Way to Freedom

Meditation, Oriental Approach
and Christian Content

by Nicolás Caballero

translated by
Colette Joly Dees

Paulist Press / **New York** • **Ramsey**

Originally published by Comercial Editora de Publicaciones as *El Camino de la Libertad.*
English translation © 1982 by The Missionary Society of St. Paul the Apostle in the
State of New York

Library of Congress
Catalog Card Number: 82-60852

ISBN: 0-8091-2476-9

Published by Paulist Press
545 Island Road, Ramsey, N.J. 07446

Printed and bound in the
United States of America

Contents

to the Blessed Virgin
to my Mother
to Those to whom no one ever dedicates anything

Preface to the English Language Edition

"I found this great treasure of real prayer and meditation so late! And so, I ardently wish that many people will discover it and enjoy its benefits." These words from a meditator using Father Caballero's approach best express my own enthusiasm for *The Way to Freedom*. While living in Spain for over five years, I spent a great deal of time and energy searching for a more authentic and enriching Christian prayer life. A seminar in Zen meditation, while revealing valuable Oriental techniques, left me with a longing for Christian content. Father Nicolás' books, with their unique blend of Eastern and Western traditions, were the answer and the beginning of a lifetime journey toward the "unfathomable riches of Christ" who leads us to his Father and our Father. Father Caballero, with his diversified background with the great mystics of the sixteenth century, St. John of the Cross and St. Teresa of Avila, and Eastern writers such as Sri Aurobindo, Krishnamurti (whose insights are often incorporated in the present volume), Swami Sivananda and others, presents a unique synthesis of Oriental techniques with a Christian content suitable for modern man. *The Way to Freedom* is a clear, uncomplicated and practical journey from our situation as *Satisfied Sleepwalkers*, to *Silence*, a gradual in-depth entry into a silence open to the presence of God, to *Meditation*, to *Prayer* and *Contemplation*, the normal and happy outcome of all the previous steps. The last volume deals with the spontaneous testimonies of two religious who have run the risk of letting go of their discursive meditation only to discover the ineffable treasure of intuitive, vertical meditation steeped in silence.

In a recent article on "Catechetics for the 1980's" in *America* (June 21, 1980, p. 518), Father Francis Kelly suggests that "after a relatively short time of discursive prayer and meditation any serious person of prayer should move on to a more passive, less word- and concept-filled communion with God in silent surrender." He deplores the fact that "young people who were never exposed to the Church's rich heritage of prayer have left us to find an alternate version in Eastern religions like Zen and transcendental meditation." Father Caballero's books present a more viable alternative stemming from the very heritage of the Church and including many valuable insights of Eastern spirituality. It is therefore with great joy that I have translated what Father

1

Nicolás has affectionately and graciously called "our book" on Meditation, and it is also his wish and mine that his other books and tapes be translated in the near future. The present volume on Meditation is so popular that it is already in its fifth edition, and the complementary tapes sold out within two months. I am deeply grateful to Father Nicolás for his confidence and encouragement, and I am convinced that I could not have undertaken this task without first experiencing the transforming liberation to which *The Way to Freedom* invites each and every one of us, lay and religious alike.

As Associate Director of the Paulist Adult Education Center at St. Paul the Apostle Church in Los Angeles with Father Joe Hanly, I have had the privilege and the opportunity to share Father Nicolás' approach by teaching two four-week courses on Meditation-Prayer. The response has been highly encouraging, with many requests to offer the course again and to use it for retreats. I believe that such a response simply indicates that many people from all walks of life hunger for what St. Paul called a "newness of life" and a "being in Christ."

Many books deal with meditation from various viewpoints but Father Nicolás' book is unique—to my knowledge—in that it offers a comprehensive and practical guide on how to meditate to the many people who do not have the opportunity to attend an introductory seminar. People who have taken the course will find in the book the reinforcement and advice they need to keep working and to understand the marvelous adventure of this gradual, ongoing process of meditation. Father Caballero suggests that a new apostolate, as essential as feeding the hungry, is needed, and it consists of learning to meditate and teaching how to meditate. It is our humble prayer and sincere hope that "our book" may show the English-speaking readers the meditative way to an authentic encounter with the inner self and with God and that it may enable them to live no longer at a level where problems are the norm and solutions the exceptions.

Colette Joly Dees
Paulist Adult Education Center
10750 Ohio Avenue
Los Angeles, California 90024
(213-474-7000)

This work represents a modest attempt to teach people who do not know how to meditate and also to help those who already meditate, as a way of seeking inner change, to improve the manner and quality of their meditation.

Within the order of inner change, of being rather than doing, of becoming, the Orient offers us very intelligent and effective techniques of interiorization. These techniques, along with the laws of human functioning and the philosophical and theological concepts, form a whole called yoga. There are different yogas according to the techniques they use and to the immediate objective which they pursue.

Today, though yoga is in vogue, many misunderstand it or are prejudiced against it, especially because they view it as connected with philosophical and religious concepts foreign to our mentality, or because they imagine it as some sort of body juggling enabling one to flex one's limbs and tie them in knots.

These prejudicial ideas aside, yoga means *union*—union with God, union with the Reality which is God. The person who reaches God reaches Reality and is fulfilled. Therefore, yoga offers a possible way to fulfillment, and this achievement improves the person both inwardly and outwardly.

In this task of personal fulfillment, meditation is the basic technique, essential to the Spiritual Exercises which I have been directing for several years within the framework of the yoga techniques of spiritual fulfillment.

In all this work, I attempt to avoid whatever may seem strange, odd or ridiculous. I consider that very careful adaptations must be made instead of mere applications—doing more or less the same thing as the Oriental does and in the same manner.

Despite my efforts to make it all clear, sometimes a certain initial bewilderment is unavoidable. It usually happens in people clinging to old stereotyped thoughts and actions. Therefore, some, though they do not understand, think they can judge the newness and the personal experience implicit in this work on the basis of their own old concepts, without any experience and, therefore, unaware of the newness involved. Others do not succeed in exploring in depth because they are so dispersed and so oriented toward the outside in their life that they would find it difficult to think that there could be other ways. Still others, guided by an emotional attitude, look with curiosity—though timidly—at something which is in vogue: prayer and meditation. Perhaps these people are not really interested in being new as the Gospel demands, but they always want new things which occupy them, though, deep down, their minds continue unchanged.

I suspect that the vogue of prayer and meditation, besides being fleeting, is reduced to a purely intellectual exercise conveyed through lectures, talks, meetings, etc. Perhaps some do not know how to do anything else. If prayer and meditation were a scientific, philosophical or theological conclusion, all of that might be helpful, but this is not so. Prayer and meditation lead us to discover, form, and preserve a spiritual reality which transforms our personal experience. The structure of this book, like those kites made of paper and reed, is simple and fragile, but it rises and enables us to rise high.

Following the first chapter, which aims at motivating people to meditate, the next five chapters present what we might call the dynamics of meditation: its nature, its objectives, how to prepare for meditation and on what to meditate. The seventh chapter, presenting some of the effects of meditation, is addressed to those who seek some assurance of success before they take the risk to meditate. The two following chapters deal with an attempt to guide those who already meditate, to forestall the difficulties they might encounter and to present a way of avoiding them. Obviously, we are not presenting all the examples nor their many nuances. This is normally left for a more personal direction.

In this simple work, I have intended to develop mainly a personal synthesis of the techniques of self-awareness and transformation in meditation. In Spanish we do not have complete and systematic presentations of yoga meditation. There are many different fragmentary studies which normally are little more than brief annotations on meditation within some isolated chapters of books on yoga. Therefore, what I present has the value of a synthesis, which I have organized and divided in such a way as to make possible an understanding of its ideas and practices. On the other hand, though a lot is being written now on prayer, nothing is said of meditation, which is a very precise technique of work with its own laws and its own dynamism. I think, therefore, that I am helping in some way to fill the gap in this area while attempting to revive, with the precise and refined techniques of the East, an ancient and effective practice that can make possible a new openness to God and bring about a change of attitudes and even of character. It offers great potential for spiritual formation, though only when we find rather perceptive educators who are capable of discernment and an openness to new ideas.

Moreover, I have situated this work of systematizing within our Christian context, relating the proposed techniques to those of mystical writers more familiar to us, especially St. John of the Cross, and using Oriental ideas when they represent a way of expressing and thinking similar to the ways of our milieu. This justifies the subtitle of this work: *Meditation, Oriental Approach and Christian Content.*

I hope all this can help people who seek the answers to life's deepest questions. Those answers will be found only in exploring one's inner self. Meaninglessness as well as boredom comes from within, as does all that makes us unclean, but there is also found the Kingdom of God, which, when given the opportunity, rises from within to give meaning to everything. God reveals himself in this inner kingdom of my own mind. Therefore, I dedicate this modest book to all those who hunger, for they will be filled with great meaning when they discover that *God is all in all.*

1 A DEFINITIVE REVOLUTION: THE SPIRITUAL TRANSFORMATION OF THE MIND (Eph. 4:32)

- *Levels of Change*
- *Your Problem is Your Mind*
- *To Meditate Cannot Be Just a Fad*
- *If You are Determined*

In regard to a course on sophrology held in Sirges and organized by the International School of Sophrology, the French reporter, Robert Barrat, noted the impact of the proclamation of Dr. Alfonso Caycedo, president of the meeting:

Meanwhile, let us be aware of what it [sophrology] represents: no more no less than the transformation of our society through the transformation of the minds of men who make it up.[1]

He expressed the impact in these words:

During my thirty years of traveling throughout the world, I have lived many historical moments as a newspaperman. But never have I witnessed the amazing sight of a man alone who announces his intention to transform the world without first pretending to take power in his hands.[2]

All things considered, sophrology only represents a new way of reconditioning the person, to enable him to live with more peace, more serenity, more discernment and less tension. And yet the revolution of

7

the mind is broader. The Gospel represents the adventure of a man alone who, by the sheer power of his whole Spirit, rooted in weakness and lack of power, promised us a human revolution over tensions, fears, individual and collected anxieties.

Levels of Change

People hunger not only for bread; without knowing it, although sensing it, people hunger for God. Where are those who can feed the crowds?

We sense the need for a change from which we hope to feel better, relieved.

- But we do not know what to change since we continually oscillate, going from the inside to the outside and from the outside to the inside, looking for culprits other than ourselves, though on some occasions we sense our own guilt.
- But even when we have situated the problem, we do not know what means we should really use to produce such a change.

This is because, on one hand, it is not easy to situate the problem, even when we note the uneasiness. On the other hand, we frequently lack the tools to control it personally. So, how can we satisfy the hunger of those who do not eat? How can we change?

Meditation is an instrument of change, providing we accept the fact that we have to change and that meditation can achieve this transformation.

When we speak of levels of change, we refer to the areas where people achieve their own transformation and to the power which operates at each level.

- On the supernatural plane, the transforming power is God, through his Spirit; the normal form of man's transformation on this plane and the *natural* way to relate is *prayer*.
- On the natural plane, within the reach of each person, the power is his own mind. At this level, the natural form of transformation is meditation through which one reaches ever deeper levels of oneself.

When we already work within a supernatural context, when our meditation directs us toward God, both levels easily overlap and we pass from meditation to prayer. Thus, although I perfectly distinguish prayer from meditation, on some occasions I will be speaking of situations where they converge and coincide.

Those two levels begin to have a practical value when we stabilize this normal swaying of modern man with his tendency

- toward the outside, attracted by what is near, by the influence of things;
- toward the inside, on many occasions called—without knowing it—by the power of his own mind and of the Spirit seeking their normal expansion.

Interiority is not exactly either the movement within or without, but the deep exploration starting in oneself and in God, within the mind, of the inside and of the outside.

At that point, prayer and meditation become a spontaneous process and we must change *inevitably*. Prayer and meditation *alter* the person. We give to this verb its original value of *change into something else*, which, in this case, is translated by:

- an alteration effected by God's presence in the person;
- an alteration which is achieved when the person discovers his *real* personality, beyond the conditionings and superficial layers which distort it. It is an authentic reaching of one's own self.

Here, the objection "Everyone is as he is," raised by ignorant people or those unwilling to risk, makes no sense. That "everyone is as he is" is a fact, but only until he becomes otherwise. We should never say that someone is hopeless; one simply has some habits which can be replaced by others.

These levels converge in the human mind and in meditation. Obviously, by meditation I do not mean the discursive kind, but something much broader referring to the activity of the mind probing itself in depth as I will explain when I deal with its nature.

The real dimension of *all* is found in meditation, and meditation takes place in man's mind.

Thus it is within that the person discovers the true dimension of things; within the person the authentic neighbor is found, and within the person is found the kingdom of God.

True happiness is within reach, but its perennial source lies within man and not without. When we direct our attention

within, and not only without, there a door opens where before a heavy wall stood. Those who learn to go through this
threshold penetrate into a new world.[3]

Within this context marked by man's greater power and his greater capacity for expansion, we find the declaration of the Second Vati-
can Council in the Pastoral Constitution on the Church in the Modern
World:

Now, man is not wrong when he regards himself as superior
to bodily concerns, and as more than a speck of nature or a
nameless constituent of the city of man. For by his interior
qualities he outstrips the whole sum of mere things. He finds
reinforcement in this profound insight whenever he enters his
own heart. God, who probes the heart, awaits him there.
There he discerns his proper destiny beneath the eyes of
God.[4]

Everything indicates that, in the process of self-growth, all levels
come together and all lines converge. This process, seen in regard to
man, is meditation, an in-depth journey into his own mind; in regard
to God, it is his free and *gracious* presence.

The attitude of those who reduce change to *thinking differently*, or
who seek to probe into their lives by *going to the outside* or by *becoming
more active,* appears absurd.

Change is an all-inclusive activity in which nothing is omitted.
Some consider it, or at least live it, in an *exclusive* way. They abandon
some things, persons, activities, places, etc., in order to take up others.
All of this contains a partial truth, but it does not represent the substance of change.

In meditation the following occurs:

- a reconstruction of the personality because it becomes more and
  more integrated;
- a new form of relationship with the environment: better interpersonal experience which involves relationship with people; a better
  use of things and a greater degree of freedom in our use of things
  and our dependence on them;
- a better relationship with God, a better prayer as we open up more
  and as our receptive capacity is expanded in that direction.

Your Problem Is Your Mind

We must recall an evident first principle: life is defined by those who live it; Christian life is problematic when Christians are a problem; religious life has no solutions when solutions are sought without a commitment in the mind of the religious person. I do not mean the conceptual mind—a conceptual revolution is a pseudo-revolution. I mean the mind in depth, which the learned of this world often disregard. Many intellectuals can describe art and even religion, but their words remain unconvincing unless their lives reflect their ideals.

It is amazing and frightening to realize how such a small, though important, part of the person like thought has managed to monopolize the whole scope of the person. It rules and defines a person. It even happens that some people identify themselves with their own ideas and ideological systems in such a way that they end up considering themselves good because they think good things. Some, though, at times, are aware of the deceit. Thoughts, the intellect, account for one-third of man's personality; the other two-thirds account for the real man.

We can say without a doubt and as a final detail at the starting point of an in-depth work:

All of man's problem in regard to his liberation is centered in his mind.[5]

Meditation will enable us to penetrate within the *entire* mind. Meditation and prayer, its normal expansion toward God, are man's unique opportunity *to become man*.

Mystics, in the broad sense of the word, are those who, with the greatest urgency, have grasped this reality. Referring to meditation, St. Teresa of Avila says:

I maintain that even if you were asking for meditation, I could speak of it and recommend it to all those who meditate—though they might not be virtuous—because it is the way to acquire all the virtues and a matter of life for all Christians to begin it, for no one, however lost he may be—if God calls him to such a great good—should abandon it.[6]

In many people's lives there exist some problems which arise directly from the impossibility of explaining the unexplainable, what lies beyond concepts, by the use of concepts. To want to experience every-thing on the basis of reason is certainly a very irrational way to live. Reason does not find its fulfillment in encompassing and explaining everything, but rather in silence, which is the normal complement of reason. Intelligent people know how to reason and how to be quiet.

The tremendous meaninglessness which many encounter in their lives comes from that and from the erroneous way of life which has its origin in this mentality.

When someone says that his life makes no sense, he must be en-couraged not exactly to seek explanations, but rather to live. The meaning of life is not found, nor has it ever been found, in explana-tions but in life itself. Such is the problem to solve—to make these people understand where to find a genuine solution.

> Intellectually I have many questions; but I always come to the
> conclusion that the way to solve them is not through reading
> or discussion, but rather through the in-depth penetration of
> my own consciousness through meditation.[7]

These affirmations pertain to someone who anxiously sought the solution of his religious problem for a long time. He was oppressed by remaining on the level of things, weighed down by what we call hori-zontalism of life. One dimension alone does not make sense, since length does not exist without width and there is no depth without the two previous dimensions.

Meditation has played a major role in all those who have sincerely sought their own transformation. Meditation opens us up to an entire-ly new world, and without it we are like blind people in a beautiful and brightly-colored world.

Krishnamurti, a radical revolutionary of the mind, whose books cannot be indiscriminately recommended except to people with basic discernment and personal conviction, represents the tendency toward the *total* freedom of the human mind. Such a freedom culminates in the silence of meditation, in the silence of the mind in the process of self-cleansing. He rebels against the idea that meditation properly done, can be a withdrawal or an evasion, an isolating and self-confining activity. For him meditation enables us to understand the world. He sees medi-tation, as our mystics did, as an authentic commitment through which we contribute to the creation of a new heaven and a new earth.

> Meditation simply observes and makes possible the most inti-
> mate mystery which occurs continually in life; it shifts one's

attention from the outside to the inside, and since that fact is characteristic of every person, far from being only a cerebral game, it gives us the most valuable aspect of our vital activity. It governs the most profound *laws of our existence* and it shapes the development of our life. On the contrary, the person who does not meditate, steeped in the outside, lives in contradiction with these laws and feels oppressed by disgust, nausea and weariness of life. He experiences with anguish a being out of place but he ignores the motive of this situation and how to come out of such misery. He has fallen outside the nucleus of life and therefore is not aware of the mystery which characterizes it.[8]

To Meditate Cannot Be Only a Fad

Fads skillfully play with people insufficiently free. The fad and its influence have a fundamentally emotional origin. There exists now an influence of all that is Oriental in our Western cultural life. Meditation is a product *rediscovered* by the West in its encounter with the Orient.

People have always meditated in the West. There are rich traditions of meditation among us. Meditation is the *normal* development of a person who grows, and so it always takes place, even in the child. But this process usually stops, and we cease to meditate and to build our own spiritual house and our own personality.

We yield to the influence of others; we think with their heads, though we consider ourselves very independent. We act upon suggestions of other people, though later we say that meditation is a form of self-suggestion. Contradiction is the normal lot of underdeveloped people. This is why they function without ever reaching a complete synthesis.

One of these current fads which is timidly reaching us now is meditation. We discover what we had lost but probably from a more serious basis, since the Orient has gone much further than we have in the West in the analysis of the human processes and of the laws which govern the human spirit, and thus the human mind.

Meditation will become truly effective when it overcomes the initial phase of being a fad. However, it will always remain an adventure, and so:

You need not travel to Burma, China or India, romantic but ineffective places.[9]

There exists a coincidence of this mentality beyond vogues and the normal scope within which a fad functions: space and time, with the Gospel which is not connected with place or time, but with the *spirit* and with *truth*.

Serious work actually begins when the person begins to be serious, which is when he becomes calm and integrated, and when he surrenders to adventure and to the evangelical risk. From that moment on, almost impersonally, the person's transformation is taking place. There is a birth of what *is*, without my having created it. Perfection is not a *product*; it is a manifestation, a birth of something which *is* and which expresses itself when given the opportunity because it is in itself *manifestation, gift* and *love*.

The deeper we go [referring to the vacuum, creating a vacuum], the more we see the soul enthusiastic and transported into love for God, without knowing or understanding from where come such love and such longing.[10]

Meditation is beginning to introduce us into entirely new dimensions. Some do not tolerate them well, especially at the beginning, which is when we oppose more resistance to the crumbling of the ideological or affective systems which we have built.

Someone was telling me once that this type of meditation is for romantic or emotional people since it fosters sentimentalism. It would have been more accurate to say exactly the opposite. What is nipped in the bud, as of the first day of practice, is sentimentalism as we enter into a phase of filtering of the affective conscious and subconscious layers of the person. At the same time a new way is slowly opening up, a new light, a new intuition, a new presence of something well worth the trouble of running emotional and intellectual risks.

If You Are Determined

In the course of several years, in my work of teaching how to meditate and to dispose ourselves for prayer, I have met many people at different levels of preparedness for this endeavor.

While some simply wanted to work, others were showing a very emotional attitude coinciding with their search for novelty, a desire to obtain emotional satisfaction or out of curiosity. Others, for reasons which were not always clear, were categorically opposed to this unusual way of working because they felt that they were losing control over themselves while penetrating within a *vague, ethereal, imprecise* milieu *without outlines.* Others were so happy with their own systems that they stuck to their ways, rejecting, violently at times, a possible way to do things better than their own way. They did not even wish to possess the basic wisdom *to try to see* if they could learn something. Basically they are people so sure of themselves, and so insecure in regard to what they do not possess, that they need to isolate themselves in their *world* and within their limited borders. This represents a seed of *counter-gospel.* Such people will probably risk very little in their lives.

I believe that a basic and at the same time fundamental apostolate consists in seeking—wherever they may be—people ready for all in order to communicate to them something which can lead them further than they themselves suspect.

It is a shame to see many souls, endowed by God with talent and grace to go further, who, if they wished to take courage, would come to this high state, and who remain at a low level of relationship with God, because they are unwilling, do not know or have not been shown the way.[11]

St. Teresa, with her grace and common sense, provides the model to penetrate in this path and to reach the goal.

Now then, dealing with those who wish to drink this living water and who desire to walk to its very source, how must they begin? It is very important . . . to have a great and firm determination not to stop until you reach it, come what may, whatever may happen, however hard the work may be, no matter who criticizes it, whether the goal is reached or you die on the way, whether you do not have the heart to keep working or whether the world collapses, as many times as you hear people say: "There are dangers," "So-and-so went astray," "Someone else deceived himself," "Another person who prayed failed," "It is harmful to virtue," "It is not for women because they build up false hopes," "They would be better off spinning," "They have no need for such refinement," "The Lord's Prayer and the Hail Mary are sufficient."[12]

There are many schools teaching meditation, but only those which recommend purification and teach how to go about it offer any guarantee of authenticity. Growth prior to the birth of a new creature is found in the beatitude of the pure of heart.

What prayer and meditation claim, what we seek therein, is the encounter with God, to see God even with the *obscure and loving awareness* to which St. John of the Cross refers when he defines contemplation, considered as *knowledge*. I am certain that the best way to evangelize others and oneself is to bring this *knowledge* to people through meditation and prayer.

With a great insight into reality, Krishnamurti warns against those who teach only *techniques* devoid of the spirit of meditation, pointing to the prior need to establish the proper foundation, namely freeing oneself from anger, jealousy, etc., while living free from fear, anxiety, etc.

All traditional asceticism recommends such purification as a necessity. It is true that meditation and prayer themselves purify the soul, but a basic minimum is needed at the start as St. Teresa warns and as all Oriental spirituality recommends:

> Now I want to declare to you—because some of you will not understand it—what mental prayer is, and, God willing, may we have it as we should. But I fear that it will be extremely difficult to obtain if we do not strive for the virtues, though not to the same high degree needed for the other (she refers to contemplation).[13]

The person who is ready for all, attempting to seek and to find the foundations—always religious—of his own life, is ready to begin meditation which, with God's grace, will lead him to self-possession and to the knowledge of God who allows himself to be discovered by those who seek him with a sincere heart.

And to the many who, without experiencing this, believe it is *hard* and *absurd*, I will tell them with St. Teresa:

> Let him who does not want to hear, go on by.[14]

2 ── NATURE OF MEDITATION

- *Meditation Takes Us to the Life of Everything*
- *To Meditate is to Penetrate Deeply within the Mind*
- *Types of Meditation*
- *Who can Meditate? When to Meditate?*

Meditation Takes Us to The Life of Everything

Everything contains surface and depth, though if we ponder this, we will realize that the separation we establish for everything comes from the superficiality or depth of the person who observes everything.

When a person begins to acquire depth, he will see the artificiality of such a distinction. It is as artificial as to oppose the valley to the mountain as if they were two divergent things. In fact, a valley exists because of a mountain and a mountain is possible because of a valley. Whoever adverts to this must necessarily admit that there can be another way of looking and seeing wherein things converge and are not opposed. This is necessarily a unifying, loving gaze.

When I do not consider the valley as opposed to the mountain but rather the necessary condition for its existence, when I see that the valley and the mountain are a unique reality, I have overcome those concrete and exclusive ways which define a valley and separate it from a mountain only according to what the eyes see and to what the superficial mind grasps. Only when we unify the surface and depth of everything can we grasp the life of all.

This is one of the great effects determined by the nature of meditation:

- Meditation is an instrument of penetration leading to the life of all.
- Meditation enables us to overcome what is fleeting and to reach what is permanent in all.

17

• Meditation destroys forms and appearances in order to reach reality.

Form is that *special characteristic of all* according to which a flower appears to us *as a flower,* a table *as a table,* a river *as a river,* sorrow as different from *joy,* noise as something different from *silence.* Metaphorically, we could define forms as the different *poses* adopted by life to present itself to us.

This, however, occurs because people relate through the senses: sight, hearing, etc. We are tied to forms by the senses and the imagination.

Yet, behind all these forms making up our concrete daily life, forms among which we also find man with his particular way of being, his character, his peculiarities—behind all this is the life of all.

That life is not reached either through the senses or imagination but solely when the senses and the imagination have been silenced.

Silence is this new quality which appears when the senses and the imagination are muted. It is only in silence that we arrive at life beyond all forms.

Meditation leads to the life of all because it is a progressive task of inner silencing. Therefore, meditation is not a means to an end but both. When one reaches the point when meditation is intense enough, it will blend with life itself. It will not be confined to a specific moment as in the beginning. Krishnamurti points out that meditation is a seeing without words or comments, a being attentive to all of life throughout the entire day. When this takes place the person creates his own inner circumstances adapted to meditation and he works at probing life and people. He changes because he also discovers *his own life* beyond the motions, waverings, ways of being, feeling and doing. When meditation enables me to discover *the life that I am,* I am already transformed and shall continue to be transformed; at the beginning, I feel ill-at-ease because my superficial layers are disappearing and a new reality is emerging. The following statement comes from the prayer diary of a nun:

> I lost my self-image. It was not real. I have the impression I worked a long time at identifying with the positive aspect of things, but I remained caught up in things and now, neither things nor God completely . . .

All is life, and God is the life of all. To change is going to mean going in search of the life of all, of *God all in all.* In that sense meditation is a basic technique for all that implies the transformation of the person because the problems we have and even the fact that we are not conscious of our essential reality, our spiritual heritage, is because our mind does not function in a totally open way; it is not attuned to what there is beyond the uproar of thoughts and mental frameworks coming from the affective level.

The stimuli coming from our body, affectivity or the external world monopolize our mental activity in such a way that we are unable to connect with what there is beyond all that world of confusion of forms.[15]

Meditation, therefore, is an intelligent attempt to reach *beyond* the forms through which things appear, and it accomplishes this with regard to God with whom we normally relate in ways determined by:

- our feelings;
- the images we have of God;
- our own way of feeling about him;
- our ideology and way of thinking about him.

But God is life and, therefore, he is prior to and beyond my thoughts, being at the same time:

- the life of my feelings;
- the power with which I imagine;
- the life which enables me to feel;
- the clarity with which I think.

St. John of the Cross' entire effort, on his way to God through progressive emptying, aims at going beyond the appearances of things which prevent us from reaching things and beyond the figures of God which obstruct our way to God:

Those who imagine God under any of these figures, as a great fire or light, thinking that what they see resembles God, are far away from him. Beginners need these reflections, forms and ways of meditation to attract them and nourish their soul through the senses . . . it must be a passing phase; they must not always remain there because in this fashion, they would never reach the goal . . . which is God.[16]

In regard to the quotation from the prayer diary which I just mentioned, I want to underline that it points to a normal phenomenon. Should we attempt to give a descriptive definition of meditation, we could include that quotation and others, and within the same context, I include my own answer to that letter:

Detachment has already begun. You have begun to get rid of that mask which we normally wear. *I lost my self-image.* God does it. In any case, do not be surprised if, at times, it reappears, because it is not totally removed that easily. However, you have begun to attack it boldly, whereas before, with all our work, we did not even notice it, but rather we strengthened it. Generally, our spirituality is very egocentric, and so, we do not grow. Here we go directly to a void, creating an emptiness for God to be able to come near us and to be our neighbor. Things do not attract you (marvelous!) and neither does God completely (normal). Read chapter 13 of the second book of the *Ascent.* Read it slowly, especially number 4 and number 5.

(Letter to a nun)

There comes a normal point when things begin to lose their grasp over us and God is not yet sufficiently strong in us. The previous quotation refers to that moment.

Meditation brings about a different vision of everything. A new world appears and this world is only accessible when one becomes new. Then the meditator begins

to feel, to share what is inherent in the object of the meditation. It is as if I were contemplating not the form of the object, but its inner strength, its inner state as if it were a living thing.[17]

To Meditate Is To Penetrate Deeply Within the Mind

Meditation, considered as an instrument of progressive penetration and of access to life—mine, God's, people's and things'—cannot occur if at the same time the penetration within the meditator's mind does not take place. We proceed from a common and plain fact explaining the very root of meditation.

I have the facts of a problem before me. Facts are dead, invariable elements. They are just present. I center more on the problem, on the facts. As I sustain my attention in that direction, something occurs: the problem appears more clearly in the light.

Actually, the facts of the problem remain without greater light or clarity. I am the one who brings light and clarity. Clarity is within me. Therefore, the whole problem is reduced to an adequate integration of its elements. The enlightenment, the clarification which take place are simply a matter of the integration which I achieve, an adequate unification involving many elements.

This phenomenon can be explained in another way. I light up an object with a low voltage lamp. The object is lighted up. If I increase the voltage, the object appears more clearly; it is clearer. In fact the light does not pertain to the object, but to the lamp. The object is brighter as I bring it closer to the lamp, to the source of light, and also as there is more light. That is, the greater clarification of the object occurs every time I place the object in the light of the lamp. Both phenomena occur simultaneously.

The same happens in meditation. As meditation brings me closer to all and enables me to see all more clearly, sharply, it is because at the same time I bring all within my own clarity, within my own mind which is clarity. Thus, while meditation is an instrument of penetration, it is also a gradual in-depth probing within my own mind, within my own light.

This principle is absolutely fundamental and it is the key to meditation.

The in-depth insight into things and people that I reach is the unmistakable sign of the depth I have reached in myself:

> Our encounter with another (and with things) occurs at the same level at which we encounter ourselves, and the other person's intimacy becomes manifest to us to the degree we connect in depth with our own intimacy.[18]

The mind lies at the crossroads of all possible ways open to man and therefore:

> Until I know *myself,* all my experiences will be lacking in their very basis.[19]

From a more spiritual, more mystical context, we have the same statement representing the entire possibility of personal development:

> So we hold that from that arid night, first self-knowledge emerges from which, as from a foundation, emerges the knowledge of God. That is why St. Augustine said to God: *Let me know myself, Lord, and I will know you.*[20]

It is normal that it should happen that way and it must be well understood for meditation to represent a fundamental value in our life.

When we project ourselves in an attitude or a way of thinking, we do so from the level of development we have reached intellectually, as well as affectively and even bodily, or, more generally, biologically. Basically:

- Because no one gives what he does not have, the light I observe in all is my own, just as the starving person sees food everywhere simply because he is hungry.
- Because no one receives anything for which he is not ready, only the things or aspects of things which I have enlightened reveal themselves to me.

There are various levels of self-penetration which the accompanying diagram illustrates:

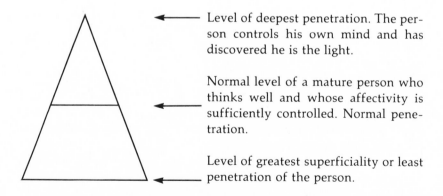

Level of deepest penetration. The person controls his own mind and has discovered he is the light.

Normal level of a mature person who thinks well and whose affectivity is sufficiently controlled. Normal penetration.

Level of greatest superficiality or least penetration of the person.

The lowest level represents someone who does not meditate at all. We could represent such a person this way:

Everything is reduced to self-satisfaction. That person certainly thinks a lot, but barely meditates. Meditation is something which takes place in quietness, in serenity. The very act of egocentric thinking, trying to use everything for oneself, is the result of a mind in darkness; it is only possible when a person does not know himself.

At the second level, the person has reached a normal stage of self-penetration enabling him to orient himself correctly in life, although without greater aspirations. The diagram of an open person describes someone at this level:

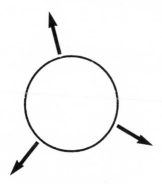

Such a person has acquired more serenity and greater self-knowledge. There exists yet another level where there are no contradictions between going outward and inward.

In the very process of meditation, as one penetrates into the mind in depth, he notices that as he centers in on himself, he is closer to everything; it seems normal to encounter everything within. It is within one's own depth that one finds a greater relation with everything. This situation, or rather this stage of the person, is shown by the point of convergence at the top of the triangle. There is no diagram because it is extremely difficult to illustrate this apparent contradiction in which, under seeming egocentrism, everything is in me, and there is the greatest openness to everything: I am open to all.

The total process of meditation, as a probing in depth of all through in-depth probing of the mind, could be presented the following way:

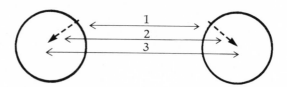

One circle stands for the meditator and the other stands for the object of the meditation.

The lines joining the two circles represent the levels of union taking place. Meditation is, I repeat, a process unifying the meditator with the reality on which he meditates.

At the first level the relation is superficial: the person has neither probed deeply into his own mind nor into the object of meditation which is not grasped. There is superficial knowledge.

At the second level, the person, having probed himself in depth, penetrates more within the object.

At the third level, the person reaches his own center and from there he can attain the center of everything. In the process of meditation, the reaching of one's center may be accompanied by phenomena of clairvoyance and insight likely to astonish superficial people. Observe how the line of meditation, shown by the dotted arrow, is a growing process of interiorization, accompanied by the corresponding arrow of increasing in-depth probing into the reality of the object of meditation.

Now we can better understand the previous statement that the objective of meditation, e.g., to reach the life of everything overlooking all appearances, is only possible through the in-depth probing of the mind in the repeated act of meditation.

The increasing understanding and clairvoyance of everything conceals no mystery. Since meditating is a gradual process of unification with all, there comes a time when the person sees himself unified with all. Therefore, it is natural that my own self-understanding means also my understanding that with which I have become one.

St. John of the Cross' statement, though empowered by grace, proceeds along this line of thought:

> Let us proceed from the lesser to the greater, from the more exterior to the more interior, until we reach the deep recollection where the soul is united with God.[21]

The starting point of incipient meditation is marked by superficiality: the person who meditates is superficial and so is his relation and contact with the object of meditation.

This initial point is often accompanied by a certain disgust especially if the person expects something to happen as the following case shows:

> I have the impression I am not doing well. Of course, I am not quitting, but I am just as I was on the first day (I have been meditating for two months which is nothing). You said that the work was cumulative. I do not see that. I seem to be climbing a mountain alone, without knowing the way, and besides with this characteristic: *I find it more and more strange and risky.* I do not see the slightest reflection of that light you mentioned. Yet, during the day, I am normally more tranquil and therefore I control the situation better.
>
> *(Letter from a nun)*

The object appears impenetrable, closed. The impression produced is often expressed by the words: curtain, brick, wall. You feel you are standing before a wall which does not open and you do not know how to open it:

> I repeated the mantra [Oriental word designating the phrase guiding meditation] for forty-five minutes and I left. It seemed like a brick. It remains that way almost every day.
>
> *(Prayer diary)*

What happens is that the mind is closed and it does not project its light upon the object which also appears closed. When you pursue the meditation, there comes a point when you feel the curtain is slightly drawn, the wall begins to open and the brick is softening:

> On that day it was not all brick.
>
> *(Prayer diary)*

The statement expresses a very normal situation which cannot and must not give the false hope that the goal is reached. At first, a certain wavering will be noticed after a while. Some slight self-penetration in the mind has begun along with a corresponding penetration in the object, but it quickly disappears because there is no stability yet. This, however, has the advantage of encouraging the person meditating and of giving him the feeling that something is taking place although he hardly notices it. At other times we notice:

> At times everything seems irrelevant or mere routine; but looking in depth, I think I am getting rid of something. I feel a little freer as if peeling off onion skins, and I have removed one.
>
> *(Letter from a nun)*

Occasionally the in-depth probing is taking place but the person who meditates is not conscious of this penetration. Yet, there are some external signs perceptible to those living with that person:

> I found this type of meditation very good. It seems to me that I am not doing anything, yet the members of the community tell me they have noticed something which encourages me to keep struggling.
>
> *(Letter from a nun)*

This is not a unique example. I could quote many other testimonies which I do not consider necessary at this point.

We cannot meditate if we reject the fact that progressive unification with the object and with oneself taking place while meditating begins with superficial stages:

> At the beginning and in all my meditations, I repeat the phrase superficially, but little by little, it penetrates more deeply until in the end, *it seems to become one with my thinking.*
>
> *(Prayer diary)*

We cannot meditate if we are not open to an unavoidable surprise when we realize that previously familiar and known things appear somewhat strange. Meditation enables us to possess the object in depth which contrasts with our usual superficial possession.

We all know the game of slowly and attentively repeating a *very familiar* word—the word "water," for example. When we repeat the word "water" slowly and attentively, it becomes *strange.* Attention has simply broken the superficial layer of the word. We manipulate things, words, concepts without paying attention to them. When we break the routine, this sensation of strangeness occurs even in the case of ordinary and familiar things. This is a meditative process, although, in this case, it is irrelevant.

When we probe in depth, the two circles showing the person meditating and the object of meditation tend to draw nearer, which is not exactly pictured in the previous diagram in which the line goes from the center of the mind to the center of the object, but by two superimposed centers: two *concentric* circles, since there is a unifying of the person who meditates and of the object of meditation.

The experiment has been conducted with a continuous meditation on *a flower.* The person goes beyond the forms of the flower becoming a flower but without forms, not seeing himself with petals, nor with the specific color of the flower, but observing in himself something which is the flower beyond the appearances: daintiness, softness. That meditation influenced his life, making it more dainty, softer. He observed that the flower was he.

The following passage from an extraordinary diary of meditation-prayer alludes to this phenomenon of unification at an elementary level:

My mind remains lucid before the object of meditation—as time goes by, it seems *as if the phrase were becoming more perceptive, something like what happens when you write with a pen; at first the strokes are light, and as you write the ink comes down and the strokes become clearer. Almost at the end of the meditation, I felt as if the phrase were filling up parts of my body:* head, arms, legs, eyes, etc.

(*Prayer diary*)

To summarize what precedes: What happens when I see the object of meditation more clearly? I am entering more into the object; I am placing the object of my meditation more within my mind, centering on it with my own light; and at the same time as I am penetrating deeply into the object, I am penetrating my own mind in depth. This delving into my own mind occurs precisely when I try to meditate, when I try to probe the object more, when I try to reach the reality and life of the object of meditation.

St. John of the Cross expresses this process of focusing on the object while centering on my own mind through a process of emptying or removing the various layers, the forms which hinder the way to reality, in this case, God:

> because we treated first the detachment of the exterior senses from the *natural* apprehensions of objects. . . .[22]

> Now it is the inner corporal sense, which is imagination and fantasy.[23]

> One must also blind and obscure what refers to God and to spiritual things, which is the *rational* and superior part.[24]

Following these successive strippings, which in fact are a gradual possession of the object as we said previously, unification with the object takes place. Such is the ultimate process of meditation, the penetration into the object.

> And so, as one enters into this negation and emptying of forms, God brings us into the possession of union.[25]

At that point, obviously, meditation is over, or, if you wish, it is the *normal* end of meditation about which we can say with Krishnamurti that it has no beginning and, therefore, it has no end.

Obviously the process of in-depth probing mentioned by St. John of the Cross is the process toward contemplation because the normal conclusion of self-penetration and penetration of the object is precisely contemplation.

Apart from the supernatural elements involved in the case mentioned by the saint, the course of in-depth probing which I am explaining in this section remains valid. When God works on someone, at least at the beginning, he does not do so outside the person's mental laws, but through their thorough use. However it may be used, meditation remains what it is:

> Meditation never ceases to be an instrument of penetration, that is to say, an instrument to possess and to assimilate reality.[26]

At the same time as it is an efficient instrument in the search for the reality of all, which represents one of the poles of meditation, its object is also from the other pole, the meditator,

the easiest and surest way to expand enhanced consciousness.[27]

However, this double process can be stopped and is in fact
stopped when the meditator clings to appearances, to the surface, and
does not allow depth to emerge. Such is the attitude expressed by St.
John of the Cross when he says:

> Many spiritual people err after having striven to reach God
> through images, forms and meditations adequate for begin-
> ners; when God wants to draw them into more spiritual inner
> and invisible heights, thus depriving them of the pleasure and
> substance of discursive meditation, they do not stop, they do
> not dare, nor do they know how to detach themselves from
> their accustomed palpable ways, and, therefore, they strive to
> retain them, wanting to go on using reflection and meditation
> of forms, as before, thinking it should always remain so. . . . It
> does not consist of working with the imagination, but of the
> repose of the soul, letting it be in quietude and calm, which is
> more spiritual.[28]

Types of Meditation

If it is authentic, meditation will always suppose:

- Penetration of the forms until one reaches life, enclosed and hidden beyond the forms.
  The goal of a good meditation also goes beyond everything
that can be manipulated, seen, felt and thought. The *normal* end
result of an ongoing meditation is always mysticism.
  Someone has even defined mysticism as a *thought thought
through to its end,* that is, until one cannot keep on thinking.
- Penetration within one's mind at the same time as one penetrates
the object of meditation. It is always a simultaneous penetration as
more profound levels of oneself are being experienced very slowly.

There are types of meditation, not because of the goal one must
attain since it is always the same, but because of the ways leading to
the goal.

These ways depend on the concept of life and of the mind which indicates that meditation is influenced by the culture and the environment in which it is born and which it serves.

There are two main cultural contexts in which meditation has a different meaning: East and West. We should understand—even in a superficial way—the phenomenon of Oriental meditation because nowadays meditation is being introduced by the influence of what is Oriental among us.

Everything Oriental is looked upon with some suspicion in our traditional religious circles generally because it is poorly understood or because of some inadequate adaptations.

The Orient is not an *exotic, mysterious* and *magical* world with undernourished fakirs sleeping on nails. More than dealing with geography or culture, the Orient deals with deeper levels of consciousness. Through its millenary dedication to the development of the human spirit in its attempt to reach God, the Orient has discovered and used with great discernment *laws* of the person, common to *all* people. We must distinguish between these laws and the techniques which embody them and the philosophies and concepts of the divine, as in many aspects the latter certainly does not coincide with Christian revelation. We need discernment and we need to abandon our emotional attitudes which make us close up or open up without seriousness and responsibility to everything coming to us.

With a good understanding, adaptation presents no problem. What is most authentic and usable from the East belongs to all and therefore there is no need to adapt it, because we Westerners also have it: it is simply a matter of *discovering* it, and then finding a way to express it in our own cultural milieu.

Two different cultural contexts give rise to different ways of conceiving life, the mind and the help the mind can bring to us. Therefore, two ways of penetrating within the mind, two forms of meditation, emerge.

In order to clarify my presentation, I am going to use a formula coming from our cultural psychological milieu. The formula consists of three letters:

$$S \rightarrow O \rightarrow R$$

S: represents the stimuli. A stimulus is what reaches a person through all the possible channels, exciting, pressuring the person in the direction of the stimulus, whether it comes from sight, hearing, etc., or from the imagination, thought, from oneself or from the outside.

O: represents the person's *inner world* and his inner *organization:* attitudes, habits, character, his way of being at a particular moment.

All the stimuli reaching the person are worked out in this area, and interpretations, motives and meanings emerge from there. For example, I receive the stimulus of a smile from someone I usually do not like. Because of this predisposition, inwardly I interpret the smile as mockery; but if the person likes me and I am aware of it, I will interpret the smile quite differently. We have presented two different interpretations, two different meanings before the same external stimuli.

R: In the two previous cases, the reaction, the behavior of the person involved is quite different. In one case, the response is rage or annoyance, in another, possibly not.

The behavior emerging as a consequence of the interpretation given to the stimuli is represented by the letter "R": reaction, conduct. The reaction, or behavior manifests itself in thoughts, words, actions, activities, organizations and institutions. Culture itself is the result of a specific way of interpreting and seeing the world, people, or groups of people.

I want to specify the Eastern and Western positions in regard to this formula.

- The East has traditionally dedicated itself to the development of this intermediary zone dealing with the person, the mind and consciousness at the level of development reached. This inner world includes the essence of what is human which the *non-directive* therapeutics of counseling defines as *subjectivity, originality* and *creativity.* This is where the *real self* dwells, where the person finds his freedom since he himself is *origin* and original, the source of all that emerges, and from where a permanent creativity and newness of the person will be possible. In this area, life is not competing nor a permanent effort to succeed, to obtain results, nor to accumulate them, all of which would imply the person's *behavior.* Here, life is understood as a state of *quietness,* repose, silence, allowing what I have and always have had to express and manifest itself. Life is conceived as a *manifestation.*

Within this context, meditation is the evolution of one's mind to increasingly deeper levels; it is a permanent and progressive self-discovery and self-possession.

The valid instruments for this self-possession are silence, intuition and quietude. Naturally, there immediately arises the possible objection of *passivity* or *quietism*. Every road to perfection has its dangers, and this is at least part of the justification for spiritual direction.

- The West has always emphasized and continues to emphasize behavior, almost exclusively. We are more interested in *doing* than in *becoming*, or rather becoming is formulated in terms of:

- accumulating;
- being able to compete;
- having everything;
- knowing how to think and having valid ideologies;
- having the strength to achieve, having character and will power.

In this area, life is an *activity*, an effort to obtain what one does not have or to keep what has been acquired. The West inexorably functions on the basis of *desire* and *fear*—the desire to have and the fear not to be able to have or to lose what one already has.

In this context, the evolution of the mind and meditation represent an effort to arrive at *results*, conclusions enabling me to change my *behavior*, to find a different way to think and to act.

The valid instruments of this meditation are: *thinking, reasoning, will power, decision* and *action*. Meditation is seen as an *activity*.

These two types of meditation represent different stages of the mind with all the consequences. It would be naive to think that one is the Oriental way of meditation, not valid for Westerners, and the other way is Western meditation. It is superficial to state that they are radically opposed and that they cannot be taken out of their cultural context. They simply correspond to two different phases of the person: the child stage and the adult stage. As one grows, the child's world crumbles and the adult world appears, although both are involved in a person's evolution. It would be erroneous to hinder evolution and to always remain a child.

The mind also has a normal evolution. Our discursive meditation corresponds to a child stage of development; Oriental meditation corresponds to an advanced stage of development. For that reason, all mystics, including ours, insist that one must leave discursive meditation to go on with another way of development. It is precisely St. John of the Cross who discovered more profound levels of functioning because he searched deeply his own mind. In his whole mental contexture, the saint is closer to the Eastern than to the Western way. The following text, among many, reflects a way of thinking rather difficult for a Westerner, and yet he was a Westerner.

And many act so when they enter this state thinking it is a matter of discoursing and understanding details through images and forms which are like the cortex of the spirit. When they do not find them in that loving and essential quietude where their soul wants to remain, not understanding anything clearly, they think they are going astray, wasting their time, and they seek the cortex of their images and discourses again, which they do not find because it has already been removed; and so they do not enjoy the substance, nor do they find meditation and they are disturbed thinking they are regressing or going astray. And the fact is, they are losing themselves, although not as they think, because they are becoming lost to their senses and their first way of feeling; this means gain to the spirituality which is given them.[29]

There is obviously more wealth in the previous quotation than what I wish to explain at this point, because the saint refers to contemplation and to the progressive action of grace. At the same time, there occurs a modification of the functioning of the person's mind which could not take place outside of a direct and clear orientation to God. To meditate in such a way, whether it be on God or on a flower, would lead similarly to such a contemplative modification, though obviously not supernatural.

Someone trying to meditate was confirming to me, very modestly, what St. John of the Cross is stating:

I have the impression I am doing nothing. I do not believe this is meditation.

After a few sessions her impressions began to change:

I think it is very interesting. Now I believe it is meditation although it is not the kind we have always been taught.

A nun was writing this to me:

I continue the type of meditation you have taught us. I have made little progress since I got into a rut because of a disappointment which was hard for me to face, perhaps because I identified with the causes of the disappointment. I do not know; besides, the circumstances around me are not very conducive to this kind of meditation [she refers to what she finds

in her community]. I try to do what I can, since I sense a great
need for this meditation.

These two types of meditation are defined:

- one by the predominance of one's activity, basically of discursive
  thinking;
- another by the progressive silencing making room for the experience of what lies beyond the appearances.

Naturally, and I wish to stress this point to avoid offending anyone, whatever system may be used, a good meditation must lead to the
same practical results. Discursive meditation will have to probe deeper
levels of the person until it leads to the end of thought where intuition
or experience arises. This is not only an effect of grace, but a require-
ment of the very nature of the mind.

I do not mean by this that one meditation is as good as another; if
this were so, it would spare me from writing. St. John of the Cross
points out that there are different ways, differently efficacious:

There are other [souls] who work hard, weary themselves and
yet regress as they make use of what is useless and disturbing,
and others who benefit greatly in repose and quietude.[30]

These two types of meditation can be graphically represented in
the following way:

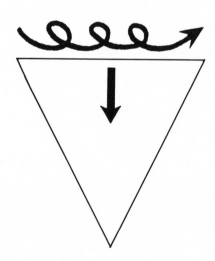

The upper line with the loops corresponds to discursive meditation which St. John of the Cross calls *discoursing and understanding details.*

It is a horizontal, extensive meditation. Little by little one reaches depth.

The vertical arrow corresponds to *intuitive* meditation which directly seeks depth although it becomes extensive indirectly.

This could be clarified with an example: one may know what there is between two distant points by going over the road between these two points, and this implies traveling, motion. Such is discursive meditation.

It is also possible to know what there is between two distant points without traveling the distance separating them, but rather by choosing a point distant enough to enable us to embrace the entire stretch panoramically, with one glance, though less clearly. This is intuitive meditation.

Intuitive meditation normally detains thinking; it stops the curved line and remains fixed on and attentive to a single point which can be a single loop of the line, as shown in the diagram:

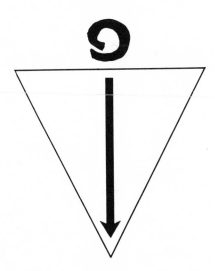

Such a meditation, clearly characterized by its efficacy and penetration in depth, requires certain conditions necessary at the beginning for every type of meditation, although they are accentuated in intuitive meditation.

The presence of these conditions determines whether one can meditate or not.

Who Can Meditate? When to Meditate?

I am constantly seeing people who do not know how to meditate, people who find it very difficult to probe in depth with a method which could transform them if it were properly used. I have repeatedly heard the comment: "This is not for me," referring specifically to the meditation which I present.

My experience over the past few years has shown me that what is not for them is something required for all meditation, which is the capacity *to be*. However, these words are too subtle or perhaps too common. It is better to say that these people lack the capacity *to be quiet*. What they are basically saying is that they lack sufficient quietude. They may be people with an overburdened subconscious.

People can meditate if they can:

- pay *willful* attention to something for some time;
- but it must be the attention of the *whole* person: body, affectivity and mind.

Not everybody is prepared to meditate at the beginning. There is a process of preparation.

The following squares illustrate the characteristics of someone unable to meditate, the characteristics required to meditate, the moment when one begins to meditate and the effects of meditation:

SQUARE 1:

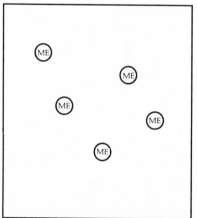

Process of dispersion
(Identification)

Square 1 shows a common state nowadays: the dispersed, dissipated person. Such a situation is due to a lack of interiority. The person has so turned to the outside and to things that he has lost his own identity, so he identifies with everything which *attracts his attention* and affects him. Such a person cannot meditate, simply because *there is no person,* because there is no unifying axis directing evolution and in-depth probing.

Such a person needs to attain some *integration,* all the more so as the level of dispersion is greater. This is accomplished by the development of willful attention which is always a factor of control.

SQUARE 2:

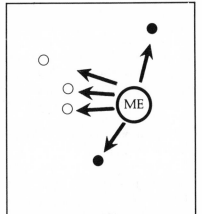

Process of control
(Attention)

Now, there begins to be a person with some autonomy and freedom. There is the beginning of a central axis which can direct and cement the evolution of the mind.

This attention begins to function *from within* the person—the opposite of what we have in the previous square which depicts attention *from the outside,* which is, therefore, *disintegrating,* because of the multiplicity of external things.

Paul Chauchard refers to the willful attention from within:

Personalizing integration is one of the main aspects of the psychophysiology of *attention,* within the field of consciousness.[31]

Then, one can begin to meditate. The initial disposition is sound. Normally, most people have this ability, although unconsciously they may always tend to the outside, unaware of their own reality.

SQUARE 3:

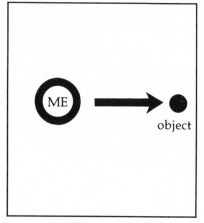

object

Process of stabilization
(Concentration)

The third square depicts concentration. In the final analysis, all attention is concentration. Physiologically, it is proved that focusing one's attention on something, paying attention to something,

> automatically causes inhibition in the basic centers, reducing the arrival of other messages to the (cerebral) edge.[32]

Logically, therefore, a person capable of *paying attention,* of *living attentively* as was indicated in the previous square, can also *pay no attention* to what does not interest him at a given moment. This is what happens in concentration. However, the basic difference between attention and concentration is the greater *span of attention* in a specific direction. Concentration

> is not an end in itself, but a means to an end. Concentration changes the mind into an instrument which one can use at will. When one concentrates, directing the mind firmly on an object, intending to go beyond the veil, to reach life, to unify this life with that of the person's mind, there is meditation. The mission of concentration is to prepare the instrument; meditation uses it.[33]

When, from among the many objects to which I willfully, consciously pay attention, I select one and stay with it, I am concentrating.

Anyone with a certain control could begin to meditate; but when one can maintain one's attention in one direction for some time, when one can concentrate, evolution and change in the direction of one's concentration begins. This already represents a meditation.

SQUARE 4:

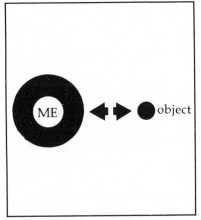

Process of penetration
(Meditation)

When the person keeps his attention on the object with the intention of penetrating in it, *penetration* occurs. This penetration corresponds to a new state of consciousness with a feeling of participating in the nature of the object.

- A woman who had concentrated on breathing felt at the beginning that she was breathing; later she told me she felt she was breath.

- Another, having concentrated on a scenery bathed in an atmosphere of peace, had the impression of a change and of an incipient experience that she herself was the scenery.

- Someone else was telling me: "It seemed as if the phrase [object of her meditation] were filling up parts of my body: head, arms, legs, eyes, etc."

                                        (*Prayer diary*)

Such is the very process of meditation. There occurs an approximation between the meditator and the object of meditation.

The fact of maintaining the mind alert and fixed upon something implies that, unable to remain in a static way, from its most profound levels, the mind penetrates the object. If the

object is another person, one begins to see him in an entirely
different way because there occurs a kind of psychic immer-
sion in that person as one penetrates within him by penetrating within oneself.[34]

This process of keeping alert in one direction so that there occurs a
fusion between the meditator and the object has many nuances and it
is highly valued in Oriental spirituality.

> When there is profound concentration and the mind does not
> fluctuate and remains focused on the chosen object, we then
> have meditation. . . . Meditation is not only a beautiful
> thought, a poetic flight or a free fantasy of pleasant experi-
> ences, but also the depth of concentration wherein the mind
> flows continuously toward a given object *as oil poured from one
> container into another.* There are not many consecutive thoughts
> about the same object. There must not be the least intermit-
> tence in the mind, so that a person will be really meditating
> when his mind is freed from all other thoughts and is totally
> focused on the object of concentration.[35]

Sivananda, a great spiritual master, expresses the same idea applied to the meditation whose object is God:

> Meditation is the continuous inpouring of a constant stream
> of divine consciousness. It is the continuous current of
> thought toward a unique object: God . . . similar to the sym-
> bolic flow of oil poured from one container into another. All
> thoughts of the world are excluded from the mind which is
> filled and sated with the thought of God, divine glory and the
> divine presence. Meditation is the regular overflow of
> thought into the object of concentration; meditation follows
> concentration.[36]

This effect of penetration occurs automatically through maintaining one's attention directed to the same point. Basic, therefore, to one's
spiritual evolution is one's ability to fix the attention in one chosen direction. St. Teresa refers to that when she says:

> Then you will say that this is already attention, that you can-
> not nor wish anything but vocal prayer, and you are right.
> But I am telling you that I do not know how to separate (if by
> praying we understand with whom we speak since it is rea-

sonable and we even have the obligation to try to pray with care); and with all these ways, please God, we pray the Lord's Prayer well and do not end up in something impertinent. I have tried it several times and I find no other remedy except to try to keep my mind on the one to whom I address my words. So, have patience which is necessary to be sisters and even to pray as good Christians, in my opinion.[37]

What belongs to the essence of a method can vary and one can choose from the various methods; however, the ability *to pay attention,* to concentrate, is not a method but the essence of all the methods.

Without the practice of concentration and meditation, no one can presume to reach the highest stage of spiritual evolution.[38]

Unfortunately, I meet many people who think they are working spiritually because spirituality attracts them. In many of them there is simply an emotional attitude often aroused by the novelty of some new religious concept, a new book or a new apostolic direction. Although it may sound harsh, they are people who live fundamentally in the spiritual context depicted in the first square. In all similar cases, we find the same clear sign of little spiritual development: egocentrism, unfortunately quite common.

I am going to point out the last square about the logical crowning of meditation, although it goes beyond the objective of this chapter, in order to provide at least a complete vision of the work.

SQUARE 5:

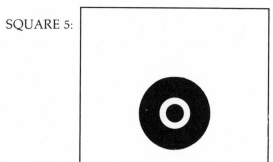

Process of unification (Contemplation)

I have no intention to explain the whole dynamics of contemplation at this point but simply to point out the progressive spiritual development within meditation. I do not wish, either, to enter into the
classic polemics about the types of contemplation and the problems
concerning the different roads to God.

I am simply referring to a phase of contemplation, direct result of
meditation which the Orient calls *samadhi.*

St. John of the Cross also considers this contemplation as a result
of meditation:

> They will have to use discourse until they reach it, acquiring
> the habit mentioned with some degree of perfection every
> time they want to meditate; they experience this knowledge
> and peace, unable and undesirous to do it as we have said, be-
> cause until they come to this stage, which is for proficient
> people, they will now use one, now the other, at different
> times.[39]

At the Congress on St. John of the Cross in 1928 in Madrid, as Angel L. Cilveti points out, a reference was made to an *acquired contemplation* directly related to continuous meditation:

> an inner, simple and loving gaze placed in God which is ob-
> tained as a result of the repetition of acts of meditation.[40]

The result is obtained when one keeps probing and maintaining
the attention on the objects of meditation. It is the result of the mind
penetrating within itself and thus also within the object of meditation.
Such is the great adventure of meditation: to lose oneself in all, to unify with all, but within oneself, which is different from losing oneself in
things, outside of oneself, as occurs with the dissipated and superficial
person.

3 OBJECTIVE OF MEDITATION

- *Why Meditate?*
- *Meditate to Change Attitudes*

Why Meditate?

We meditate, first of all, to become persons. The solution to the human problem is not in *doing*. Doing is only the manifestation of a previous level, a mental level, a level of consciousness where doing takes on meaning and direction.

Meditation serves to penetrate this mental level, to become more conscious and *to act* more meaningfully and with more consciousness.

However, since God has a saving plan, a plan of relationship with man, the latter must place his meditation, his mind—which is all he has—at the service of his divine vocation.

For God has called man and still calls him so that with his entire being he might be joined to Him in an endless sharing of a divine life beyond all corruption.[41]

When meditation arises from this objective, it is religious meditation. The mind can go in different directions, thus giving rise to several types of meditations:

- Philosophical meditation dealing with *virtue, goodness, beauty, unity, being.*
- Psychological meditation which is directly aimed at a change of character, a change of attitudes.
- Religious meditation whose finality is God. The two previous types are included in this meditation since God is Goodness itself, Beauty, Truth, Unity and Being.

Simultaneously, the entrance into this world through mental penetration, modifies a person's character.

Therefore, the definitive objective of meditation is religious.

Then, upon entering into relationship with God, a new element, profoundly modifying the human mind in its transformation, comes into play, and that element is *grace.*

The mind serves adequately to penetrate the essence of a flower until contemplation, to reach a person's subconscious and even to read its thoughts, but it is entirely powerless *to reach divine life beyond all corruption through its efforts.*

Religious meditation, the mind at the service of divine vocation, serves to *open us,* only to prepare us to welcome this superior life when it is given.

Religious meditation, with which we are dealing, sets the divine in first place and the mind in second place. One loses importance in meditation; the beauty of meditation is meditation itself.

Meditation is this state of silence, beatitude and manifestation which occurs when the person is beyond his own conditioning: when he does not cling to his body, affectivity or thoughts. When he breaks through these limits, a new panorama appears. The person who has no place in meditation is the one who wants to enter into it without letting go of the bonds which tie and limit him. That person is not important in meditation.

When meditation occurs, when the person is open, even though the person is important, he is not the most important. What is most important is what one opens up to: divine life, the whole truth, the very goodness of all, total beauty, life beyond death.

Meditation serves this religious goal. Such a meditation is intimately related to the process of personal *salvation,* an effect of grace, of one's liberation or openness to God.

The objective of this meditation is salvation conceived as a *total* fact and not only the salvation of the soul as we have often thought in the context of a partial and ineffective spirituality.

For the human person deserves to be preserved; human society deserves to be renewed. Hence the pivotal point will be man himself, whole and entire, body and soul, heart and conscience, mind and will.[42]

Such is the whole objective of religious meditation: to attain divine life, to know God with the *whole being*—body and soul, conscience, intelligence and will.

We are no longer dealing solely with the penetration of the mind as we pointed out earlier, but with a new penetation occuring when

Through the gift of the Holy Spirit man comes by faith to the contemplation and appreciation of the divine plan.[43]

In this case, meditation, the meditator who penetrates his own mind, opening up to stages of greater consciousness and lucidity, makes room for and welcomes the Spirit of God who renews him:

Through this Spirit, who is the pledge of our inheritance (Eph. 1:14), the whole man is renewed from within even to the achievement of the redemption of the body (Rom. 8:23).[44]

Through the combined power of the mind and grace, meditation fulfills its goals of introducing man into a new atmosphere from which he emerges with a new wisdom *surpassing all meaning.*

Today's great apostolate, as necessary as feeding the hungry, is to meditate, to teach meditation, because we all *need God's glory.*

The intellectual nature of the human person is perfected by wisdom and needs to be. For wisdom gently attracts the mind of a man to a quest and a love for what is true and good. Steeped in wisdom, man passes through visible realities to those which are unseen. Our era needs such wisdom more than bygone ages if the discoveries made by man are to be further humanized. For the future of the world stands in peril unless wiser men are forthcoming.[45]

The final objective of meditation is, then, progressive spiritualization:

- through the power of the mind, one's spirit opening up to itself and to a superior manifestation;
- through the power of the Holy Spirit who *renews all, searches all even the depth of God.*

Spiritualization is a process of love.

- The mind, as it penetrates deep within itself, is unified beyond all selfishness in a place where egotism does not exist. And amour-propre, which is a kind of superficial, interested and defensive union with oneself, is replaced by a more profound and purer union: authentic self-love.

- The Holy Spirit unites us with God, giving birth to our love for God.
- A growth of love for our neighbor occurs because this personal renovation by its very nature and that of man, is transcendent, leading us to interpersonal relationship and to society as pointed out by the Council in *Gaudium et Spes* (n. 3).

I have many meditators' written testimonies alluding to this reality. Here is one of them:

I have realized that love is the goal of man's life, the goal of meditation, a unique love encompassing God and men in one single reality. I realize that we are all important and that we are all One. Throughout the day, when I remember, I become conscious of *this* and I really marvel; it leads me to other people. What concerns me is that I cannot maintain *this* during the whole day, and with the rush, the comings and goings, it fades away.

(*Prayer diary of a boy*)

As we have gradually explained, the objective of meditation is self-penetration of the mind, total salvation and love. It is an explosion of love which does not experience separation.

Meditate to Change Attitudes

Man understands himself through his attitudes. God's salvation within someone becomes clear in the attitudes which a person expresses.

If we consider meditation as work to be achieved and not only as a theory which we must know, we must see it as working toward a change of attitudes. We receive grace when we open up to God, but openness is *an attitude.*

We need to be intelligent in our effort to belong to God, which does not mean that we should be *calculating,* since we would easily eliminate the normal *risk* inherent to the Gospel. To be intelligent means to know the dynamics of a change of attitude, since this is what we are dealing with.

It is rather naive to say: *you must try;* you can *if you want to.* You can get off the track, or, as St. John of the Cross indicates, you can work hard and inefficiently in spite of good will because of a bad way of working.

An attitude is a situation or a state of the whole person which means that in every attitude there will *always* be:

- a corporal element: basically the nervous system and the muscular tone;
- an affective element: feeling well or not feeling well, likes or dislikes, joy, peace, serenity, aggressiveness, fear, apprehension;
- a mental element: ideas, judgments, prejudices, the values and meanings I give to things, events and persons.

Meditation seeks to:

- create a new muscular tone, to live less tensely, to create a better functioning of the nervous system, more unified and controlled;
- create a better way to react, to decrease sensitivity, to depend less on the impression or uncontrolled impact of things, to increase the tolerance level, the capacity to withstand frustrations, to attain habitual serenity and peace and to eliminate aggressiveness and irritability;
- create new meanings, new values, with which all reality can be enlightened.

Meditation tends to change directly, to penetrate or deepen the inner life, the inner organization from which emerge the meanings attributed to life, people, things or events. A change of attitude conditions:

- The meaning of the incoming stimuli. For example: if a person I like does something unpleasant to me, in all likelihood *it will not upset me,* or at least not as much as if I dislike that person. Everything comes to me with the meaning that I myself place there.
- The number of stimuli reaching the person. The inner attitude predisposes to see uniquely that to which I have become sensitized and not to see what does not interest me. The inner attitude is a normal factor of *selection* of the incoming stimuli, or, perhaps, in everything one sees only that toward which one is predisposed. Such is the meaning of the New Testament's words: "To those who love God, everything serves for good," simply because such people are oriented to God's goodness so that they see it in everything, even there where others see just the opposite. Indeed things take on the color of the glasses through which one looks. Therefore, it is essential to rule and control the glasses, although they are not obviously the ideal which consists rather of living without

glasses, pure and open to all without distorting anything. Such is certainly the best way to live and to control the situation. I will deal with this later.

• The conduct or answer a person adopts when urged by the stimuli. Take a gesture I have interpreted as being scornful. My behavior will correspond to that meaning; I will be upset and I may react with a long face, sharp words or silence. If, on the other hand, I consider it to be a funny face, my reaction will be very different; I may smile, or even if I think it is a sneer, I can work it out inwardly with the proper attitude and consider that God loves me and is testing me by allowing me to be offended. If my attitude is authentic, in this case also, my behavior will be authentic and correct.

We can say, therefore, that man's whole problem concerning his liberation is in his mind.

Inasmuch as we transform our mental attitude, we will transform our vision of problems and things, our perspective of ourselves and of others; our capacity for understanding, initiative, mental flexibility, etc., will develop.[46]

The externalized mind, with habits and attitudes oriented to the *external world* and to *self-defense* sees unpleasant *things which happen* as problems; but as we penetrate the mind and create more profound attitudes, we will observe that humanity's problems are not the things which happen, but the way each one of us feels about *what happens*. So, while for some death is a problem, for others it is a solution because our problems are projections of the problems we have not been able to solve in our minds.

When will man understand that his *only* salvation is in a change of the mind by means of meditation and its normal outcome, contemplation?

4

PREPARATION FOR MEDITATION

- *What Many Do Not Know*
- *External Preparation*
  1. Posture
  2. Time to meditate
  3. Place for meditation
- *Internal Preparation*
  1. Preparation of the physical level
     (a) Breathing
     (b) Relaxation
  2. Preparation of the affective level
  3. Preparation of the mental level

What Many Do Not Know

To prepare for meditation is more than just preparing the substance of meditation. It involves, above all, an *attitude,* a life style encompassing a person's whole environment.

A meditator is conditioned and limited by:

- A body with a specific structure determining the temperament; an affectivity and a sensitivity to the incoming stimuli; a mental structure and mental content stemming from the very experience of life.
- The environment in which a person evolves, lives and expresses himself; an environment which is the person's projection and prolongation.

It is increasingly clearer that I am *myself and my circumstance.* It is ever more difficult to separate the person from his surroundings and more artificial to ignore the connection between what we call inner and external life without a break or lack of continuity. Man is the one who lives, what he lives and his way of living it.

In this context, the preparation for meditation is the attempt to harmonize the whole meditator's environment.

- We must seek inner harmony because there is no inner unity until we create it. The various sectors—body, affectivity, mind—have developed unevenly, whereby we may find a young body, infantile affectivity and an adult mind. The imbalance which occurs physiologically can also occur with life.

  Meditation certainly brings harmony to the meditator; nonetheless there must be some minimal sense of harmony at the start to facilitate spiritual evolution, and this is what we call *internal preparation* for meditation.

- One must be in harmony with the environment. This is an extremely important factor in the person's whole development. The environment conditions development and expresses it at the same time. To seek harmony with the environment is what we call *external preparation* for meditation.

  Later on, one notices that, more than a being-in-harmony with the environment, the external preparation signifies the *absence* of the environment, a calculated absence which the East calls *pratyahara* or *withdrawal*. The goal is to seek the origin and the meaning of the environment at its very source: within the person.

  This whole process of harmonization is absurd if one does not aim at:

- A progressive renunciation of whatever slows down spiritual progress: envy, jealousy, enmity, etc. If there is no initial detachment, a desire to be free from all this, it is better not to start to meditate, for it will only bring disappointment.

- A burning desire for *liberation, fulfillment, betterment*. As I will indicate later, many people do not progress because they do not ardently desire it. The following anecdote taken from an Oriental context, expresses how realistically we are to understand this.

  One day a disciple sought his master and told him: "Master, I wish to find God."

The master looked at the youth with a smile. The youth returned daily, claiming that he wanted to consecrate himself to
religion. However, the master knew well what to expect.

On a very hot day, he invited the boy to accompany him to
the river to bathe. As the boy was diving in the water, the
master followed him. Grabbing him by the head, he held it
under water for a good while until the youth began to struggle to get his head out of the water. The master let him go and
asked him what he really wished for while he was unable to
breathe in the water. "Air," answered the disciple.

"Do you desire God in the same way?" the master asked. "If
so, you will find him immediately. But if you do not possess
that desire, that thirst, you will never find the religion you
seek despite your struggling with your intelligence, your lips
and your strength. As long as you do not experience this
thirst, you are worth no more than an atheist. In fact sometimes, an atheist is sincere and you are not."

When this total harmony exists, concentration and meditation will
be possible. Meditation is a penetration which takes place and follows
concentration.

Success in meditation implies the mastery of concentration
and of all that builds it up, bodily relaxation, momentary indifference to what happens nearby or far away, emotional
calm and sharp vision. A man seated on his chair in an attitude of concentration is seemingly asleep, but the active consciousness of his brain is more alert than ever. In meditation,
this powerfully alert consciousness is focused on the subject
of thought. Meditation is the opposite of sleep. It deals with
the regular flow of thought to an object upon which one concentrates without difficulty.[47]

Thus we find an environmental, corporal, affective and mental
meaning of the preparation for meditation, all at the service of a very
precise and ardently desired goal. The final result is a pacification of
the person. Once we are capable of quiet attention, we can initiate
meditation.

External Preparation

External preparation includes:

- the bodily posture for meditation;
- the hour or time to meditate;
- the place for meditation.

1. POSTURE

It must be the most adequate and comfortable. However, we must specify that the most seemingly comfortable posture is not necessarily the most comfortable according to physiological laws. Sitting in a comfortable armchair can be *very uncomfortable* for the body. A *comfortable* posture is one which can be maintained for a long time *without need to change.* It may be pleasant to sit in an armchair for a while, but soon the body requires a change of posture. When the body tolerates a posture for a long time, it is because it does not impair bodily functioning. This, then, is the most suitable posture for the body.

On the other hand, the best physiological posture must allow a better functioning of the nervous system, freeing it and preparing it for meditation.

Though there are many schools and nuances in Oriental spirituality and about the way to practice, they are almost unanimous in regard that the most suitable posture for meditation is

- *sitting* (not lying down). They indicate various sitting postures easily found in books about physical yoga. For most people this is mere gymnastics. To make it more natural and normal within our Western mentality, one can sit on a chair.

  The characteristics of the chair are extremely important. Not all chairs are physiologically suitable or equally useful. In our case the chair must be neither very high nor very low, approximately seventeen inches high so that one sits at a right angle. This is depicted in the following diagrams:

- Correct chair, neither too high nor too low. The soles of the feet are firmly on the floor.

- This chair is too high. In this case the body tends to slide from the chair in the direction of the arrow. One will naturally resist that tendency by making an effort in the opposite direction. This effort may be so slight that one is unaware of it, but the subconscious tension either affects or prevents concentration. The meditator may be surprised by his failure, but the cause is very clear. I recall the case of a short person who selected a low chair to meditate. I warned her that I thought it was too low, but she answered that she liked it and it felt very comfortable. It so happened that she was unable to meditate. I asked her to change chairs, and to her great delight she was then able to meditate.

- This chair is too low. In this case the raised legs raise the knees and the thighs, which causes abdominal pressure impairing breathing. The normal breathing in meditation is called abdominal or deep or diaphragm breathing occurring in the lower part of the lungs. This is the normal breathing when lying down.

  The pressure from the legs in this area impairs breathing, and this combination prevents one from attaining a soothing rhythm, suitable for meditation. One does not calm down, nor concentrate, or at least not the way one could by following the norms.

Back of the chair

Shape of the spine

- The back of the chair also plays an important part. An unsuitable chair can hurt the back and make meditation difficult or impossible. There are various suitable shapes.
- A low back reaching the first lumbar vertebrae. In this case, it serves as a symbolic support preventing one from slipping back. The whole spine is almost free. With this small support, after a few days, it becomes easy.
- A back as high as the dorsal vertebrae. This presents no problem since the entire spine is supported.
- Normally a back with a 30° angle suffices. Then its height is unimportant. The previous backs were *straight.*
- The *head, neck* and *trunk* must be straight but not rigid. The balance of the body is assured by keeping straight. In this way when meditation begins to leave the body free and tranquil, the body will not tend to collapse as it does when one falls asleep, and the nervous system functions better.
- The *hands* simply rest on the legs or together on the lap, with the right hand, palm up, resting on the open left hand, without clasping the fingers to avoid the slight pressure which their being clasped would produce. Some people find it useful to rest their hands on their legs palms up; this is better in the summer, because hands that perspire can be disturbing in meditation.

In the beginning when we come out of meditation, it is common to feel some slight pain in the back, or the neck at the level of the cervical vertebrae. We should not be concerned, as it will disappear after a while. Eventually we will enjoy this posture which is good for the body and in which physiological laws are respected and a better functioning of the nervous system is assured.

2. TIME TO MEDITATE

We must respect each person's possibility. Nevertheless, there are advisable hours and others totally unadvisable. We should seek first what is possible and then what is best.

The best moments to meditate normally mark the passage from night to day and day to night. At those hours the body is usually better disposed. Many people, especially in religious communities, will find it easy to meditate during these early hours since, according to their rule, this is the hour designated for meditation.

It is strongly unadvisable to meditate after meals, as one can experience stomach pains because the physiological activity of meditation does not agree with the digestive process. One must wait several hours until digestion is completed.

One should not meditate before going to sleep. If meditation immediately precedes night sleep, in some cases I have found that people are unable to sleep. Meditation activates the brain and produces the very opposite of sleep, as sleep is fundamentally based upon a cerebral inhibition and inactivity.

3. PLACE FOR MEDITATION

It must be without noises, quiet and pleasant, with clean air if possible, and with the least amount of noise. If noises cannot be entirely avoided, they should at least be familiar and monotonous so that the meditator might get used to them and cease to notice them.

The room temperature should not be too low. Feeling cold can prevent concentration and meditation. High temperatures are equally detrimental. The body must feel comfortable and in harmony with the environment. It is important to look for a place with these attributes and to remain in the same place in order to establish a continuity between the meditator and the place of meditation.

When a person disposes himself to meditate at a given time, on a suitable seat, and adopting the proper posture, the external preparation for meditation is completed.

Internal Preparation

The entire preparation is one of harmonization as we previously indicated. The same process must now take place internally. Preparation does not only precede, but it goes with meditation to the point of becoming part of it. It is a work of unification in which we seek the greatest possible convergence of the body, affectivity and mind at point *zero*. The following diagram illustrates the direction that preparation for meditation itself must follow in search of progressive unification.

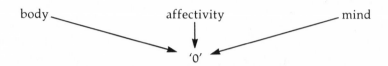

Internal preparation is a progressive, gradual *unification* of consciousness. This means that the body does not seek its own objectives; that affectivity does not disperse consciousness by going after its tendencies, likes or dislikes, guided by imagination or memory; that the mind can settle where it chooses and remain alert in that direction. To unify consciousness means that there is a single point of reference—meditation—and that the body, affectivity and the mind converge on it. Meditation is possible upon achieving unification.

From this way of viewing the internal preparation for meditation, it follows that meditation will not be the same every day, but more and more intense. This gradual unification is a good sign of progress.

More concretely, the unification of consciousness signifies:

- For the body: corporal senses. We become aware of many things through the body. We need this consciousness to guide and organize ourselves under the many incoming stimuli. Although in this respect the mind exercises a certain selectivity, noticing one stimulus and not noticing others, nonetheless this selectivity does not succeed in suppressing the dispersion assailing attention and consciousness through the senses. This dispersion must be reduced to point zero.
- For the affectivity: the things which come through the senses or which we imagine have an *impact* on us. They affect us more or less. As before, there is dispersion: many things affect us with a certain intensity; they affect us more or less. The fact is that all that affects us destroys our quietude and alters our serenity. We must resist the impact of things, persons and situations.

    We must come to the point where we are affected only by the object of the meditation.
- For the mind: there exists an inner speech which must be gradually reduced.

We give a name to each level:

- *Physical consciousness* for the consciousness we have through the senses.
- *Affective consciousness* for the consciousness we have of the *impact* produced by things, persons and situations.
- *Mental consciousness* for the consciousness of the inner speech, its content, meaning and relationship.

To unify consciousness is going to mean stripping each aspect of consciousness of its own objects or to reduce them considerably.

- We will gradually suppress the objects of the senses at the level of physical consciousness until we are left with less dispersed and more strengthened consciousness. We achieve this by corporal silence, basically produced by relaxation.
- We prevent the affective consciousness from being affected by inner stimuli, memories, images, etc., or external stimuli: people, things, events coming through the senses.
- When we succeed in doing this we recover *consciousness* which is not uniquely affective; we achieve greater clarity and a greater capacity for observation. There is less dispersion obtained through affective silence. This silence depends partly on the previous and partly on the following silence.
- At the level of mental consciousness we reduce the thinking process, the inner verbalization, the inner word we are constantly uttering. Thought, expressed in words, is silenced when verbalization and inner chatter cease. We obtain this through mental silence.

Point zero, previously mentioned, is therefore the silence of the body, the affectivity and the mind. To come to this silence is gradual, from one extreme of the line of the diagram representing the greatest noise of each person, to the suspension of all noise in the body, affectivity and mind.

When we reach point zero we will have only *consciousness*, alertness, with *nothing* in concrete. At this point meditation becomes contemplation, with some confusion and vagueness, but with utmost alertness. St. John of the Cross refers to this with the acute perception of an Eastern *yogi* when he says:

The soul desires to be alone, its loving attention centered on
God, without specific consideration, in a state of inner peace,
quietness and repose without any activity or exercises of the
faculties, memory, understanding and will, at least not discur-
sively which consists of going from one to another; rather in a
state of imprecise, loving attention and knowledge, as we say,
without any specific insight and without adverting to its object.[48]

Meditation and preparation lead to the point where we lose sight
of everything except consciousness, clarity, and awareness. As I mentioned earlier, at some point, preparation merges into meditation itself.

I am quoting the following excerpt from a nun's prayer-medita-
tion diary, very rich in content, to point out some level of unification
of consciousness and its manifestation in the symptoms which the religious mentions:

I noticed that I was being more submerged in God. I did not
notice that I was breathing; there came a moment so intense
that I did not know if I was sitting or in the air, if I had arms
and legs. Before such an occurrence and whenever it happens,
I have the impression of being asleep. (How does one distinguish?)
When the half hour rang, I entered again into depth *with the
impression that God with a capital "G" was so close to me that I could
almost feel his breath, and a great light within my mind.*

1. PREPARATION OF THE PHYSICAL LEVEL
Nobody can meditate if he is tense. To prepare at this level implies
a tranquilization of the person, a calming of the functioning and attaining corporal rest through relaxation and controlled breath.

(a) Breathing
Breathing is a world of its own related to the physiology and the
affectivity, and, through them, also to the mind and consciousness.
Naturally, given the extent of this work, we are not going into more
details at this point. Physical life and psychic life are as closely related
as the two sides of one coin. For this reason internal situations will affect breathing, and the alteration of breathing somehow conditions a
person's affective life.

The suitable way to control breathing in preparation for meditation consists of what we call *reducing the length of the breath.* In exhaling
always through the nose, the outcoming flow of air continues for a certain distance. The length of breath refers to the distance traveled by

the air when it comes out of the nose until it disappears. The longer the flow, the more active, tense and excited is the person. When this flow decreases in length, calm, serenity and quietude increase.

If one wishes to meditate, the first thing to do after sitting the correct way is to control breathing.

The following diagram schematically shows the inhalation always through the nose, and the exhalation also through the nose.

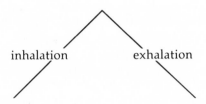

inhalation   exhalation

Begin breathing out all the air in the lungs. Exhale until you notice you must make an effort to get rid of more air. Then stop. Everything must take place effortlessly.

Now inhale *as slowly as possible* but without effort. When you notice you must make an effort to take in more air, stop and begin to exhale *as slowly as possible* without letting any air escape. You yourself release the air little by little, slowly, as you control its coming out.

Make sure it happens smoothly, in a continuous flow without jerks or interruptions. When you observe that you must strain to exhale, stop and begin again to inhale.

It is extremely important to concentrate at the same time as you do the previous exercise. The object of your concentration can be:

- The very air you take in and breathe out. Follow it as if you saw it enter and leave.
- Or the movement which occurs in the body, the up and down movement of the chest, the up and down movement of the muscles involved in breathing.

This second point of concentration works out best for many people.

(b) Relaxation

Relaxation plays a direct role in the initial process of isolation or withdrawal of the senses from their own ends. The Orient calls it *pratyahara* or withdrawal or abstraction.

This is obtained by eliminating tensions. Most of us are usually tense and we contract the muscles unnecessarily, which implies fatigue and a decrease of the energy that we could devote to something else. When a person is tense to some degree, consciously or unconsciously, the mind endeavors to maintain the muscular contraction. If we succeed in relaxing the muscles, we will have at our disposal greater mental energy freed from its role of maintaining the contraction.

Such a contraction is a waste of energy always at the expense of consciousness losing its lucidity and clarity.

All of this may appear very subtle from the outside without entering into this system. We normally live grossly, without refinement. Some may think they already meditate well without any concern for all of this. What I am saying is simply for them to do it better, with a better use of their own resources and with the outcome of a more effective meditation and attitude change.

We need to locate the tension points. Tensions frequently accumulate in the following points:

- eyes and forehead
- mouth, tongue, throat, lips
- jaws
- neck
- nape of the neck
- shoulders
- arms and hands
- legs
- solar plexus (pit of the stomach)

To meditate we must relax the body properly and loosen muscular contractions, like someone who would undo the ocean waves leaving the ocean smooth.

This form of work seems to contradict the need to incorporate the body into the spiritual life; it might seem that we are trying to get away from the body, to get rid of it. Yet, because of this seeming absence of the physical level, the nervous system gets back its power and its ability to allow the highest states of consciousness because we know that the mind functions through the brain, through the nervous system. This is indeed the best way to blend what is physical and spiritual. Moreover, a serene, relaxed body reflects much better the spiritual experience of meditation in the normal context of daily life to which it turns after meditation.

Consequently, the nervous system begins to regenerate itself. We cannot sufficiently stress the *decisive* importance of that system in a *person's human maturing.*

Although it is advisable and many times necessary to do the relaxation exercises under personal guidance, I am nevertheless going to give some indications to help people locate and loosen their tensions.

The basic rule stipulates *never to strain* to relax. Evidently making an effort causes a new tension. The ruling principle in relaxation is the mind with its power *to model, to give form* to the body. For example, when I am sad, my sadness is reflected in my body and more specifically on my face, or when I think *I have a lump in my throat* and I become paralyzed. The mind, through ideas, has a quality called *ideoplasia. Ideo* concerns ideas and *plasia* is related to plastic, plasticity, which means *to give or take form.* Ideas can shape, give form to the body and produce alterations under adequate conditions. In fact to relax the muscles is to give them a new shape, a new plasticity. The appropriate conditions are:

- To pay attention, to concentrate on the part of the body we want to modify.
- To maintain the idea we wish to see take shape: in this case, muscular relaxation.
- The inner attitude is *to let it happen,* to let what I suggest happen without making any effort.

With these basic ruling principles, sit down for meditation in the posture already indicated.

- Now concentrate on your feet and your legs.
- Do nothing; simply keep concentrating, *observing* how *they are relaxing, loosening up.* Allow some time for your thought to take shape. If it does not happen at first, remain tranquil. It does not matter at all.
- Go over all the points previously mentioned where tensions may build up.
- Observe your hands and your arms. See how they loosen up, how they relax, how they are becoming very, very heavy. Do everything very slowly, without rushing.
- Let your shoulders drop. Do not raise them.
- Now concentrate on your jaws and let them be relaxed, limp. Your teeth will separate and perhaps your lips also. It does not matter. Notice how your face feels rested.
- Now relax your throat and observe how it becomes loose.

- Let your tongue float freely in your mouth.
- Now pass on to the nape of the neck, for many the most common place for tensions. Many headaches originate in this sector.
- Go to your eyes now and proceed the same way. Many people find it difficult to relax their eyes. If such is the case, first become aware of the meaning of eye tension and do the following:
- Close your eyes forcefully, tightly. Then observe the tension which is this tight sensation which you are now noticing.
- Now slowly, little by little, relax these tensions. Since you created them willfully, remove them in the same way, but slowly. Those involuntary tensions difficult to suppress alone and directly will be followed by the conscious loosening up of the eyes after a while.
- Then loosen up the tensions of the forehead and the scalp in the same manner.

When you have finished, especially at the beginning, you may notice that tensions have returned when you stopped focusing on them. It is advisable to do this several times before each meditation. After a while, it will require less time and relaxation will be more lasting until it becomes permanent and continues throughout the meditation. Later still, it will last during the entire day and you will observe a new form of life, a new way to respond and even to think due to the decrease of the pressure of muscular tension.

2. PREPARATION OF THE AFFECTIVE LEVEL

Affectivity is the hobbyhorse of most people. Apart from physical circumstances such as illness, cold, excessive heat, etc., the real and profound causes making meditation difficult or impossible have an emotional origin and they proceed from a conscious or unconscious level.

To allow meditation to take place, this level must be controlled and pacified. The following sketch shows the situation of affectivity within the person's structure and also facilitates the direction to adopt in the work to control it. The nature of the union body-soul has always been and will continue to be an enigma. We are not interested in solving this problem within the context of this work. For us the interest resides in our knowledge of this union, or mutual influence, verified in recent years by *psychosomatic* medicine dealing with a person's physical ailment, which is a bodily reproduction of a psychic ailment, a patient's mind inadequate way of being.

The Oriental is aware of the repercussions of the affectivity in the body as well as in the mind; he notices that whenever the affectivity is altered, breathing and the muscular tone are also altered. Hence this highly suggestive sketch:

It indicates that the body and the mind are mutually influenced by affectivity (the psychic aspect) and by breathing and relaxation (the physical aspect).

You can also observe that affectivity, breathing and relaxation correspond as the two sides of a coin. If we control one, we necessarily control the other, and if we control this intermediary zone, we control the body and the mind.

This is all we need to organize the reconstruction of a person's affectivity and to influence the mind and the meanings it creates. The elements most easily controlled because they depend upon a person's will are precisely breathing and relaxation. All of this means that when we prepare physically for meditation, we are already preparing the emotional level to a great extent. In fact, with relaxation and more restful and slow breathing, serenity and peace, previously nonexistent, are also appearing.

As we reach ever deeper levels of relaxation and as more effective breathing occurs, we will notice a more profound calm which will even pervade our daily life.

The explanation of this whole influence of relaxation and breathing upon our affectivity follows: Affectivity has direct and immediate repercussions on breathing. This fact is easily verifiable. But the process also works the other way around: if we control breathing, we can control the affectivity and inner calm and peace are created.

Affectivity totally influences the muscles increasing tension or *muscular* tone. An excited person notices directly those muscular signs or their changes in terms of circulatory changes or rigidity or some other of the many ways in which affectivity manifests itself.

We could compare the repercussions and connection between the affectivity and the body to a movie projector. The projector projects the image on the screen. The image is the expression of the affectivity;

the screen is the body: nervous system, muscles. If we gradually remove the screen from the projector, the image continues toward the screen, but it is more blurred and unclear upon reaching the screen. There will come a point when the screen is far enough from the projector, and although the projector still provides light and projects the image, it will not be visible on the screen. Yet, no one will doubt the fact that the projector continues to send the lighted image.

In a similar way, when we achieve relaxation, we are taking away from the affectivity, the power to be translated in symptoms which are what the excited person feels. What excited us before will eventually meet a relaxed body, and when that happens, the emotion will not be seen as such. Lacking the symptoms, it will simply appear as an idea, without strength. If a person achieves an atmosphere of relaxation, which is perfectly feasible, this person will also be capable of keeping a low level of excitability and consequently a higher level of control and peace.

Thus, the preparation of the affective level coincides to a great extent with the preparation of the affected level, namely, the body.

As we insist on the daily practice of these exercises, we obtain something we knew, but only as a concept: serenity which usually astonishes those who meditate.

In the same way a specific emotion is destroyed: fear which so impairs spiritual life and the emergence and expansion of one's depth. Depth only manifests itself in an atmosphere of confidence and security.

The emotional state most detrimental to meditation is, without a doubt, fear—not the fear of something concrete, but the crystallization of the insecurity an individual has felt and feels within himself before life. This fear, with its many ramifications and its multiple disguises, continually interferes with whatever a person undertakes.[49]

This fear which is born of the imagination and the person's special inner organization, sustains that organization and thus prolongs this state of fear.

I have spent many years in learning the mind's secret operations. The power of the imagination inflicts real damage on the mind. Imaginary and multi-faceted fears, exaggerations, mental ruminating, castles in the air, all this is caused by the imagination. . . . A lot of energy is wasted on these ungrounded fears.[50]

Affectivity lies in the border zone, or rather it is the outcome of the body-soul encounter. When the body relaxes, affectivity is much more controlled, although not entirely, since sometimes tensions proceed from incorrect mental factors, erroneous meanings and interpretations which prevent a peace rooted in corporal relaxation from becoming stable. Peace will come when, besides modifying bodily tensions, there is a change in the mind's evaluations conditioning the appearance, the intensity and the positive or negative sign of the emotions.

When we initiate this task of tranquilization by breathing and relaxation, it is useful to concentrate on this feeling of soothing and peace which is taking place.

An interesting complementary exercise before meditation consists of seeking harmony with everything, with heaven and earth, the inside and the outside, becoming conscious of one's own peace and wishing it to everyone. A pacified person is in harmony, silent and on the way to greater harmony and peace. To be at peace means to be ready for meditation. Later, meditation itself prepares for greater depth.

3. PREPARATION OF THE MENTAL LEVEL

To tranquilize the mind means avoiding the deluge of pressures and contents proceeding from the affective level.

As one becomes serene, all there is in the mind originating in the affectivity decreases little by little.

Mental contents consist mostly of:

- thoughts
- images
- memories

Turning back to the sketch on affectivity, we observe that the mind is influenced by the stimuli coming from the body and affectivity. When the mind depends heavily on body and affectivity, it is in a state of constant agitated thinking. In such a case we find little inner silence and much chatter.

The body-affectivity link indicates the way to bring tranquility and silence to the mind. The very fact of relaxing and becoming serene provides agreeable mental silence. Obviously it is not yet total silence, since all inner chatter or verbalization does not depend on the body or the affectivity. The very nature of thinking imposes a certain rhythm and mental activity. Total silence will directly result from the continued practice of meditation, as the following excerpt from a prayer diary indicates:

In my morning meditation of a magnificent text from St. Augustine, I repeated the phrase: *I loved you too late, O ancient beauty forever new, I loved you too late.* The phrase itself was long, but I believe I only *repeated it mentally four or five times* and *then I became rapt in it without commentaries as when you see something beautiful and you keep looking at it open-mouthed.* I noticed great calm and serenity in the meditation.

A few days later the same person wrote:

For approximately fifteen minutes I focused on the word *God,* in a few seconds of total silence, simply gazing.

This silence, outcome of the intensive and continuous practice of meditation, is explainable. Let us consider a thought, each thought appearing in the mind as an ascending line

originating at a point "A" which represents a sort of vacuum, since we do not know from where it comes. This thought follows its course to "B" where it disappears. Immediately another thought begins with the same course, and so on. The course may vary in length, but the fact is that every thought begins and ends of itself.

I want to underline the fact that between a dying thought and a rising thought there is always *silence,* a blank zone.

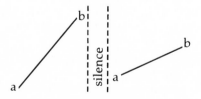

It is not a matter of understanding the nature of that silence, always beneficial, but of pointing out the fact and its great importance for meditation.

Progressively as meditation continues, the silent space expands.

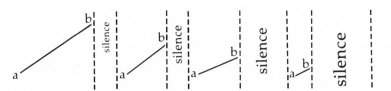

It is hardly noticeable at first. All thoughts seem welded and cling-ing together without any space between them. Then, slowly and pro-gressively, we begin to notice the intermediary world of total silence. Each thought becomes shorter and the silence longer. The meditation, which originates in this silence, is improved by silence; it is increasing-ly more profound, contemplative and transforming.

Although this involves the effects and results of meditation, we are still within what we call preparation for meditation. As I men-tioned earlier, preparation is not the same every day; it becomes more profound to the point that preparation eventually merges with medita-tion, and meditation prepares itself.

I conclude this chapter concerning preparation with the following beautiful quotation indicating the attitude of a person ready to medi-tate:

Meditation is one of the means of learning the art of leaving the body in full consciousness. Having obtained the invari-able stability and fixity of consciousness, the attention gradu-ally withdraws from the outside world and from the body; the senses are tranquil while the mind is intensely active, with all its concentrated energy, internally ready to launch into an idea, the most profound idea possible, while it works on the physical brain.[51]

5   MEDITATION METHOD

- *Change your Method of Meditation*
- *Concentrate on an Object*
- *Learn to "Look" and to Be Silent*

Change Your Method of Meditation

This obviously applies to those who already meditate. To those who do not, I say: Meditate with the least amount of fatigue and the greatest benefit.

There are methods and systems of meditation. However, our criteria for selecting one or another way are usually determined by taste, education and our information. Not all the methods are equally effective nor does the required effort always compensate the results:

> It is a shame that some souls work hard, weary themselves and yet regress as they make use of what is useless and disturbing; and others benefit greatly in repose and quietude.[52]

Most common systems usually function by using the mind *extensively* based on discourse: discursive meditation graphically illustrated by the line

This type of meditation, founded on thinking, is naturally effective, but less so, and it requires a greater effort. Moreover, it pertains to a less perfect stage of development.

Many spiritual people err after having striven to reach God through images, forms and meditations adequate for beginners; when God wants to draw them into more spiritual inner and invisible heights, thus depriving them of the pleasure and substance of discursive meditation, they do not stop, they do not dare, nor do they know how to detach themselves from their accustomed palpable ways, and therefore they strive to retain them, wanting to go on using reflection and meditation of forms, as before, thinking it should always remain so.[53]

There is a method of meditation in a *straight* line which

does not consist of working with the imagination, but, in the repose of the soul, letting it be in quietude and calm, which is more spiritual.[54]

In the previous quotation, St. John of the Cross obviously refers to contemplation which is the normal outcome of meditation, since meditation is the way to reach the calm and repose to which *reflections* lead (cf. *Ascent,* II, chapter 12, n. 7). I present them here because they refer to a fundamental characteristic of the *straight line* method.

This method bypasses *reflections* and *discourses.* Yet it is meditation, because *it is not the goal,* but a *means* still as St. John indicates. Moreover, this method with contemplative characteristics is followed, since we succeed and penetrate in depth as we attain the *repose of the soul, letting it be in quietude and calm with loving awareness.*

We might call this form of meditation "intuitive." Since we are dealing with God, we must naturally clarify the word, because God is not the object of intuition but of contemplation. We might speak of meditation with some aspects of contemplation to which it leads rapidly with less effort and more effectively.

Both methods could be illustrated thus:

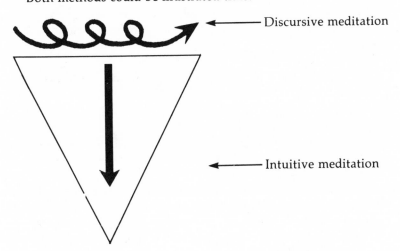

The looped arrow represents discursive meditation in extension which eventually gains in depth, but with more time and effort.

The vertical line shows meditation in a *straight line.* Its technique consists

> of the sustained fixing of the mind on a reality in order to penetrate it, to actualize it in the person's consciousness.[55]

The key lies in stopping the discursive process. One focuses solely on the object of meditation, maintaining the attention on it as we are going to explain in detail. This is rooted in a basic law:

> The law of the mind is such that one can become what one intensely thinks.[56]

What happens is that the object on which one intensely focuses occupies the consciousness, filling the mind.

> If an idea occupies the mind exclusively, it takes on an affective, physical and mental form.[57]

Dealing with the person's spiritual transformation, Sivananda's practical application takes place:

> If, then, you fill the mind entirely with the thought of God and only of God, you will soon come to a state of perfect ecstasy.[58]

God, nevertheless, can enter one's consciousness in discursive meditation,

> striving to reach God through images, forms and meditations,[59]

or this can be reached more quickly when people

> learn to be in God in quietude with loving attention and alertness.[60]

If we understand this mentality of a Western saint coming from our Christian milieu, with evangelical revelation we will have no difficulty in accepting the intention which runs through this work: to adapt the Oriental methods of meditation in the West, attempting to use their techniques within our mental context. I say this because, except for the Oriental theological and philosophical concepts with which we are not dealing because they are *perfectly separable* from the techniques, St. John offers an active method of work based on mental control and the purification of the faculties. Mouni Sadhu says:

> The Eastern methods of meditation are based first on the control of the mind and secondly on the purification of the heart.[61]

To control the mind means:

- To concentrate, to bring the mind from dispersion or attention to many things to sustained attention on a single thing.
- To suppress the entire intermediary world interposed between the person and the object of concentration.

What is interposed between the person concentrating and the object of concentration is:

- the incessant inner chatter which must be silenced;
- the desires which must be emptied and purified.

The method rapidly leading to depth and to the contemplation of the object of meditation comprises:

- *concentration;*
- *becoming silent* which we will call *learning to look.*

Concentrate on an Object

Concentration, learning to concentrate, is the great means of self-control and transformation. It is a vast and important subject deserving of separate treatment; here we simply underline its importance. Meditation only begins when one begins to concentrate and not before.

When the mind concentrates on something and continues to sustain that attention, an approximation begins to occur between the person and the object of concentration. Meditation is this very process of approximation. When this approximation has run its course, one will reach the end of meditation which is contemplation.

The fact of gathering strength and bringing its total weight to a given point, or an object, an idea, an action forms the process of meditation. Applying this concentrated force gives it the greatest efficacy with the least amount of time and effort.[62]

To concentrate means a gradual quieting of the mind, an attempt to stabilize it. This is partly achieved in the preparation for meditation, as I indicated earlier.

To start meditation a person must remain:

- with a serene mind;
- with a relaxed mind;
- with the sustained determination to penetrate the object on which he wishes to meditate.

When the preparation is over, when the person is relaxed, enjoying some degree of peace, he will notice *less difficulty* in focusing only on a phrase, an object, an idea. Gradually it becomes *easier* to sustain the attention on a single object and the mind does not run after something else. By using this system and the described preparation we achieve what many never achieve with all their tense efforts. For example:

When I learned to concentrate in order to meditate, I discovered the meaning of what the Lord is saying in his Word almost by intuition. I noticed it on very rare occasions before, after extraordinary efforts to concentrate and to empty myself, and now it powerfully surrounds me, making demands on me and exhorting me.

(Prayer diary of a nun)

Although the following chapter will deal with the object of meditation, I can now take a phrase from the Gospel or the New Testament such as "God is love" or any other phrase whose content I wish to make mine. Let us not forget that meditation is a progressive unification with the object on which I meditate.

When you have disposed yourself for meditation:

- being relaxed, serene, tranquil, you must focus on the phrase without tension, and without strain,
- and repeat it *mentally,* slowly.

At that moment two normal things take place:

1. The feeling that nothing is happening; the idea that what you are doing is a waste of time and that the phrase *means nothing.* It is like a brick.

This is the time to recall that, at the beginning, the person is very dispersed and therefore superficial. When we focus on something, we cannot penetrate deeper than we have within ourselves. But as we go deeper in repetition and center on the object of meditation, we will penetrate deeper in the phrase. We will notice that it slowly invades us, telling us something, and it slowly stops *being like a brick.*

Gradually, this phrase [God is love] heard and read or spoken so many times, on different occasions, was acquiring another nuance; it is no longer a beautiful saying but a Someone, alive, personal. . . . Once more I realize how with a single phrase my whole life is being unified; I can transform my whole life with regard to God and to my brothers.

(Prayer diary of a nun)

2. The consciousness of distractions, our difficulty in concentrating the mind.

This phenomenon begins to appear forcefully when we are tranquil and when we focus on something. This situation saddens people anxious to work and meditate well. They are disturbed when they notice that instead of decreasing, distractions increase, or at least they appear to increase.

They may certainly increase, although what normally happens is that one becomes aware of each and every distraction, which, along with the desire to avoid them, causes more anxiety, and they stand out more.

St. John of the Cross warns that it is impossible to avoid distractions in the first moments of contemplation. They belong to the normal process of a person's development:

In recollection the imagination usually flutters about.[63]

Sivananda offers the correct solution in this case:

During meditation, impose no strain on the eyes (very important warning) or the brain. Do not fight the mind; relax. Let the thought of God flow gently. Ponder the object of medita-

tion unwaveringly. Do not react violently against meddling
thoughts. Sustain lofty feelings, and what is vitiated will vanish by itself.[64]

Everyone working at spiritual achievement has experienced this
which means it is not a matter of being deficient or abnormal. It is simply the result of a superficial mind as is the case for most of us. On the
other hand, distractions do not hinder the process if we know how to
handle them.

The great Hindu philosopher and mystic, Aurobindo, refers to this
situation of the person and his consciousness. When a person is not
wholly unified, he is conscious of an inner sector unrelated to the object on which another sector is concentrating. When this happens, consciousness may remain in the silence of concentration or foreign
thoughts may float about unnoticed.

When distractions appear, *do not resist them.* When we resist them,
we then use the part attentive to the object of meditation diverting it,
in order to become attentive to the distractions, or to the distracted
sector in which case we have total distraction. But if we do not resist
them, simply letting them *come and go* without struggling against them,
then distractions *occur* as something impersonal, as if they were external. In that case the person is attentive and distracted at the same time.
It is difficult to comprehend this phenomenon without having experienced it. People do not understand how one can be simultaneously attentive and distracted. The inner interplay is more subtle. One sector
of the mind is quiet, attentive to the object, while the other sector, the
distracted sector, appears as a background, as an impersonal "It is raining, snowing, cold." The attentive part is certainly aware of the distractions, but it does not see them, nor look at them. Aurobindo calls this a
reasonable success.

Gradually as one continues to penetrate the mind in depth in meditation, the absent sector is incorporated to and unified with the attentive part. A unified mind is taking shape, and it is totally centered on
the object and on the directions of its fundamental and unique aspira-
tion. By then, all distractions have vanished.

It can and does happen that, initially, a person abandons his meditation entirely dragged away by the object, person, idea or distracting
image. Do not become impatient but calmly return to the object of
meditation a thousand and one times. Here is some useful advice:

We must accept that inevitably the mind wanders; because on
the mental level, we are infants, and we should not be dis-

mayed when the mind loses track. When someone is in pain
and gets mad because the mind is distracted, it means his self-
esteem is way out of proportion. Let us be sensible and accept
the fact that we are not experts from the beginning and that
we must learn slowly. When we learn, we normally make
mistakes, and each time we react to the error we take a step
forward in the learning process. It is not therefore a matter of
nerves, or getting mad, but of patiently going back time after
time with all due patience, hundreds of times if need be.[65]

Learn to "Look" and to Be Silent

There exists a distraction, which I mentioned earlier, consisting of
going to *something else.* It may be and it so happens that, even while focusing on a particular thing, a person is distracted. This is another form
of distraction. When one is focusing on a single thing, without leaving
the object, one is normally *thinking.* Although this may seem too subtle,
that person is distracted because thought separates him from the thing
on which he concentrates. I see the thing through my thought of it.
Then thought is an authentic distraction. This is the meaning of Sivananda's words:

Concentration increases as the number of thoughts decreases.[66]

Concentrate on any object: a pencil, a holy image, a flower, a face,
etc. You will observe that you are speaking internally. In fact, you are
not seeing the pencil, the image, the flower, the face. You simply pay
attention to the ideas, words which you internally associate with these
things.

Try now to look at the same thing again without saying anything
inwardly. Despite the fact that it is difficult, it is perfectly feasible, and
when you really achieve this, you will possess an authentic treasure.
When I relate to something without inner chatter, this relationship is
direct: it indicates an experience of the object, weak at the beginning of
meditation, but progressively more powerful and profound. This silent
looking, unencumbered by distracting thought, is our only solution.
And this solution is for everything. It can become a lifestyle in our relation with everything and everyone. If we really look without verbal-
izing, without giving names, we will experience things and persons
directly for the first time.

This is the real and fundamental question: *to acquire the authentic freedom to look.* If we observe, we will notice that it is a *direct* look without any intermediary, and at the same time it is a *silencing* of all that lies between the person and the object. Evidently as this silencing takes place, I look more directly at the object, which gets closer to me since the distractions leading to other objects and the thoughts separating me from the object lessen.

This being so important, I present the following diagrams, going from total distraction to total concentration: they represent the path followed in meditation, a path we must learn:

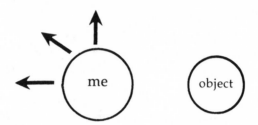

This represents someone totally distracted. The person centers on something different from the object of meditation, although perhaps only at times.

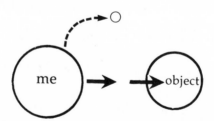

This person is distracted and attentive at the same time as was previously explained. This implies progress and it is the normal situation of someone who begins to meditate.

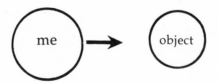

This depicts a person entirely attentive to a single object but with an intermediary world. One is separated from an authentic experience of the object by:

- Ideas through which one sees the object.
- Past experiences making one compare what happens and what one sees at a given moment with something already past. In this case, one does not really see nor look at the object but one's past experiences. This object only serves as a screen to reflect the past.
- Analyses, the hows and the whys, all the questions asked in relation to the object.

All of this represents the inner chatter, one's internal verbalization which makes it difficult to have an authentic experience of the object of concentration.

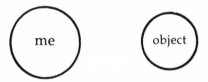

This diagram shows the silent person with nothing separating him from the object. This situation corresponds to the *full experience* of the object. The person and the object merge, and we call this *looking*.

The following quotation from a religious exemplifies what I am saying. It corresponds to an advanced phase of meditation. There are no distractions separating one from the object; the person is concentrating although there exists that more subtle distraction: one's own thought. In this specific case even that thought or this inner chatter vanishes, though only briefly and not yet permanently:

I felt freer than ever from everything which helped me concentrate more on meditation. Over half an hour had passed. I was repeating the phrase more slowly until finally I remained hanging on a single word, "God," lengthened, pondered, tasted. I do not know what is happening but it seemed as if I were falling within, in the depth of a great mystery never completely revealed with always more to discover. When only the word "God" remained in me, it seemed that all that could be thought, said, discovered about him were concentrated there. Then, usually, *I say nothing. I only look.*

(Prayer diary of a nun)

We normally function according to this plan:

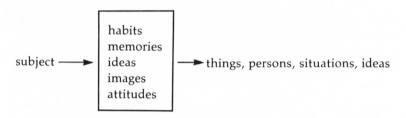

We see and live our whole world of things, persons, situations and ideas through this intermediary world made of habits, memories, previous ideas, images and attitudes.

A person who functions this way builds a shell so thick and so unnoticed, through which he sees everything, that he will experience very few things in life although he may think otherwise. His experiences will in fact be reduced to:

- comparing
- judging
- interpreting
- deducing
- etc.

Such a person does not see, does not experience, but simply relates what he sees with what he saw before.

Discursive meditation involves this whole intermediary world; intuitive meditation tries to eliminate it. This is the great difference and characteristic of both methods. From this perspective one can easily judge the respective importance of each meditation.

In reference to God, this intermediary armor prevents us from going directly to God. Our ideas and thoughts of God can turn into an obstacle to reach God. Hence the great insight of St. John of the Cross is emptying, silencing, enabling one to reach this utter simplicity whereby one sees things, without any intermediary space, as if it were for the first time.

The space is all this world which separates. If we suppress it, the seer and what is seen merge and the space disappears to give way to union. Although St. John of the Cross speaks of inner silencing, learning to see as a result directly related to the contemplation of God, it is still useful to achieve a more perfect knowledge of everything. Referring to God, St. John says:

> To receive this divine light more clearly and abundantly, take care not to interpose other more tangible lights or knowledge or figures of any kind.[67]

When we begin to look at something without anything in between, everything appears in its own light; nothing is destroyed or distorted by our own ideas, feelings, and previous experiences, nor by prejudices. This intermediary world not only contributes to distort the world in which we live, but it also distorts the reality of God. For this reason, St. John continues:

> When the soul is purified of all sensible images and forms, it will bathe in this pure and simple light, and through it be transformed.[68]

This false inner world, which prevents one from looking and being unified with everything, stems from the desires, likes and fears, ideas, memories and prejudices. Renovation will not be possible if this intermediary obstacle is not silenced.

To clarify what preceded let us examine how two people look at rain. One planned to go on a trip and cannot because it is raining; another was distressed because it had not rained for a long time and the earth was dry. The fact is that neither of them has really seen what rain is. They have simply considered what rain is *for them,* which is the same as saying: what rain is, seen through this intermediary world. People usually identify with this intermediary world, and therefore they say "for me." One sees it as a curse, the other as a blessing. Yet, what is rain when one looks at it without an intermediary obstacle? What is rain when one looks at it without desire or fear? In all certainty, it is neither the rain of the one who does not want it nor that of the one who does. When one really looks at it, without looking through *anything,* is when real meditation takes place, in the ecstasy of truth.

On the other hand, the person who does not succeed in casting inner chatter aside is a *closed* person, unable moreover to really see or look at anything with objectivity. No one is open because of his ideas on openness, but in his capacity for inner silencing enabling him to see everything without any intermediary. A closed person's characteristics are:

- Tension and a certain slant on the physical level.
- Affective agitation. He becomes conceited if you praise him, sad if you criticize him.
- Inner chatter. Absence of silence.

Such a person cannot look and cannot, therefore, meditate, although he can discourse up to a point. He will not even be able to see the simplest thing without introducing his own complication.

On the other hand, an open person is silent and the person who has reached silence is open. Openness represents a reality of the whole person and not only of thought.

If all of this seems very subtle, it is because we are distant from ourselves and unaccustomed to observing and distinguishing our own inner states. Our introspective faculty is impaired and we cannot change our attitudes or direct the spiritual progress for which we long.

Learning to look enables us to become intuitive, to contemplate, to have new authentic experiences and consequently to change. The changes modifying this inner world without silencing it are not authentic. Genuine change stems from an experience always following silent looking. Thus the only genuine change proceeds from *meditation,* whether it be centered on our own depth, that of the world, or of God, with the condition that we approach these worlds in *pure simplicity* and *poverty of spirit.* As a summary:

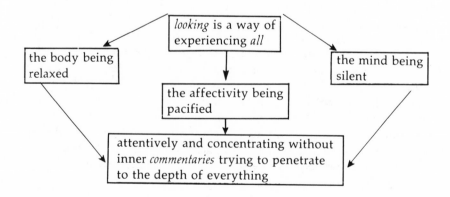

The following exercise taken from the Oriental tradition is very easy and very effective as an initiation in the practice of mental silence. Look:

- Look fixedly at a black spot on the wall. If you get distracted return to the spot and look at it with the desire to see the spot without saying anything internally.
- Look at an image—Christ, the Virgin—or look at the tabernacle. Try to penetrate within that image or object, avoiding all inner chatter. You will notice a new manner of looking, a new influence.

Listen:

- Listen to any noise and do the same as above. Avoid inner verbalization; simply observe it without tension.
- If you hear a disturbing noise, it is because you interpret it as disturbing. Stop talking and listen to it, and you will notice that it is inoffensive. If the noise prevents you from sleeping, notice that when you become silent, although the noise may continue, you will fall asleep.

Observe:

- Observe your thoughts inwardly in silence without getting irritated by them. Let them come and go without getting involved. Separate yourself from them as someone looking at something from a distance.

Such a silence is not only demanded for prayer and meditation, but it is also necessary for one's own psychic reconstruction. The following lines from St. John of the Cross express this reality which psychologists should learn to use wisely:

Even though you may not benefit as much from this void as by losing yourself in God [this] is very much worth doing to free yourself from many griefs, afflictions and sorrows and in addition to free yourself from imperfections and sins.[69]

As we have suggested earlier, words condition our looking, and when we approach things with our ideas, feelings, fears, etc., we will obviously be unable to see them. This is the great technique of our own transformation.

We normally speak of what we are, but we are also what we verbalize, not always what we speak out, but what we speak inwardly. St. John of the Cross expresses it in a Christian context:

The work of the soul consists of loving God, without wanting to feel or see anything. Thereby, passively, God communicates with it.[70]

Beyond attentive silence to God, God certainly comes and the mind is transformed *from light to light without wanting to feel or see anything,* because that too is speech and lack of silence.

For all this essential and effective work, we must create a wise pedagogy leading from external silence pertaining to the preparation for meditation unto internal silence which is part of meditation and its outcome. In the following passage from Pope Paul VI, we notice this progression from the most external to the innermost silence.

In order to understand the religious problem, we need silence, inner silence, which presupposes some external silence. Silence: we mean the suppression of all rumors, all the sensible impressions from all the sounds our milieu imposes on us and which make us extroverted, deaf while filling us with echoes, images, stimuli which deaden our inner freedom to think and to pray. Silence does not signify sleep; in this case it means a dialogue with ourselves, a tranquil reflection, an act of awareness, a moment of personal solitude, an attempt to recover ourselves. We will even add more, we will give to silence the capacity of listening. Listening to what? To whom? We cannot say, but we know that spiritual listening enables us, if God gives us his grace, to hear his voice, a voice easily distinguished in its sweetness and strength.[71]

6 THE OBJECT OF MEDITATION

- *On What to Meditate?*
- *How to Meditate on an Object*
- *How to Meditate on a Phrase*
- *Ways to Meditate Repeating a Phrase*
- *How to Meditate on a Quality*
- *The Happy Outcome of Meditation: Silence*

On What to Meditate

Meditation must have an objective, a goal. One meditates to change one's attitude in the direction of personal necessities and this necessity to change *in a direction* determines the object of meditation. Let us then call the object of meditation that on which our attention and concentration are centered which also points to the path to be followed towards personal transformation.

It is possible to meditate without a fixed direction, but it is not advisable, and neither is it good to have *a meditation for each day of the year* because, despite the fact that meditations with changing objects produce some results, they do not usually allow focusing in depth in the direction of personal change.

Therefore when we mention the possible objects of meditation, we do not mean that one can go jumping whimsically from one to another. To stay with one well chosen object is *essential.*

The possible objects of meditation are:

1. *An object:*
- A person (seen or imagined): image, Christ, etc.
- An object (thing): a flower, garden, candle, etc.
- A scene, situation, event: the crucifixion, a person begging, an accident, etc.

2. *A phrase:*
- "God is love."
- "I loved you too late, O ancient beauty forever new, I loved you too late."
- "In God we live and move and have our being."

3. *A quality or abstract idea:*
- Peace, security, humility, life, etc.

These are *simple* objects which can be combined and give way to a great variety of objects of meditation.

The following diagram shows the possible arrangements which can be made with the simple objects of meditation.

We call *formula* the various forms which the object of meditation can take under the various arrangements.

	1	2	3
	Object	Phrase	Quality
1. Object			
2. Phrase			
3. Quality			

To determine the formula, notice that the object of meditation can be repeated in a vertical and horizontal line preceded by numbers from 1 to 3. It works very simply.

The object can be considered:

- Alone with the corresponding formula 11 which is the point of convergence of the vertical and horizontal lines 1-1.
- With a phrase upon which one focuses at the same time as on the object. The corresponding formula is 12.
- Simultaneously one observes in it a quality, or rather one looks at the object and sees it through the quality which permeates it with the formula 13.
- Or one can look at an object (1), reflecting a quality (2) while repeating a phrase (3). In this case the formula is 123.

The phrase can be considered:

- Along with an object with the formula 21.
- It can be centered on objects. The phrase becomes concrete, but it disappears as a phrase. The formula will not be 21 but 2–1 which means that the phrase has been replaced by concrete objects.
- It can be used alone: 22
- It can be reflected in a quality; then it is 23.
- Or it can be a phrase (2), plus the object in which it becomes concrete (1), plus the quality reflecting the phrase and the object; hence the formula is 213.

The quality can be considered:

- Concretely seen in object: 31.
- Within a phrase: 32.
- Alone (corresponding to meditation without forms): 33.
- Concretely in an object with an accompanying phrase while looking at the object: 312.

For clarity's sake, I am giving an example of each formula not to suggest jumping from one to another, but only to present all the various possibilities.

Object:

11: A Christ (seen or imagined), a scene, a flower.

12: While I contemplate Christ I repeat: "My God and my strength."

13: As before I contemplate Christ but under one aspect, when I observe a particular *quality* in him: generosity, or will power; or I can see a scenery reflecting peace.

123: While I see an object: Christ seeing his quality of strength and repeating the phrase: "My God and my strength" or "Give me strength."

Phrase:

21: While I repeat the phrase, for example, "God is love," I see it take shape in something which expresses that love which God is: a flower, a scenery, a person, a concrete poor man, etc.

22: The phrase alone repeated indefinitely. The Oriental calls it "mantra," and its repetition "japam." To do japam is to repeat a mantra or phrase indefinitely, as for example "God is love."

23: It is the same as before but now the phrase reflects a quality. If, for example, I want to meditate on strength, I make up or seek a phrase referring to that quality as the biblical phrase: "I will be your strength."

213: A phrase depicting a quality is projected in an object in which the quality is seen. Looking at the object seen with the quality, I repeat the phrase. For example: "God is love" expresses love, which I can see reflected in a flower that I contemplate, as the expression of love which is God and of his love for me.

2-1: This formula refers to the phrase when it takes a concrete shape in an object without repeating the phrase. For example, the previous phrase becomes concrete in a Christ whom I contemplate without repeating any phrase. I see the phrase realized in Christ.

Quality:

31: A quality, for example, *peace embodied in a peaceful person's face:* image of Christ, a peaceful scene.

32: I repeat a phrase which reflects that quality: "I leave you peace; my peace I give you," or "God's peace surpasses all things."

33: I meditate and concentrate directly on a quality without making it concrete and without repeating anything: Peace. This is a very advanced meditation which the Oriental calls meditation without forms. It is difficult and not advisable at the beginning.

312. This is the combination of a quality seen in a person, thing or event, while repeating a phrase involving this quality. For example: I look at a serene and peaceful scene while slowly repeating: "Lord, give me your peace" or "I am your peace."

These examples give a sufficiently clear idea of the possible object of meditation and the variations it offers to the meditator.

This clarification helps us understand that we are not dealing with a rigid and enslaving scheme. One can meditate on anything as long as the object of meditation is intelligently selected. It will serve as a guide toward one's own mental probing in depth. Once the mind has reached depth, it will be able to go to the depth of any object of concentration immediately.

All of this means that at first it will be necessary to remain persistently with a *unique* object of meditation. Again the object can be a thing, a phrase, a quality or any of the possible combined forms, but, once selected, it must be preserved continuously.

Within the dynamism of meditation the object appears as something alive, although not necessarily at the beginning. It is essential to keep this in mind to avoid the initial moments of meditation when everything appears petrified, when nothing happens. I will come back to this later.

When I spoke of the gradual penetration of the mind in dealing with the nature of meditation, I indicated that meditation is a simultaneous progressive penetration of the mind and of the object. This slow but gradual and certain penetration of the object is what causes the sensation of a live object. Its appearance changes as the mind passes from the surface to the center. Vivekananda, an Oriental mystic, refers to the path which must be followed:

> When through previous preparation the mind becomes strong and controlled and when its perceptive ability is sharpened, it must be applied to meditation. This meditation must start with dense objects, and it slowly ascends to finer things until it becomes meditation devoid of objects.[72]

In this meditative process the object becomes progressively simpler. There is greater interiorization with a gradual destruction of the *forms* under which the object appears.

If I start to meditate on an external object, I am looking with my eyes open but gradually I feel the need to close them. The object then loses its visible forms and it stays as an image which indicates a higher degree of interiorization. Gradually the image itself disappears leaving only an experience, a *general obscure knowledge* of that object.

We can begin meditation by repeating a phrase, and gradually the phrase vanishes, giving way to silence.

We need not worry about traveling that path. The path simply manifests itself. We must simply let ourselves be guided and led along the path itself as long as it seems *practicable.*

The object of meditation may seem *too* simple, but since simplicity only upsets complicated people, it will only be difficult for people considering quantity and complication as signs of efficacy. I invite them to let go of their structure and inner complication to surrender to weakness. St. John of the Cross foresaw this gradual simplification:

> I would like to persuade spiritual people that this way to God does not consist of many reflections, ways, manners or pleasures although beginners may need them.[73]

The attitude of evangelical simplicity wherein God effects his own *manifestation* is found within this context of greater simplification and simplicity.

How to Meditate on an Object

As I have previously pointed out an object (persons, things, events) is the simplest and easiest form of meditation, which does not mean that it is the most elementary form of meditation. That depends not upon the object but upon my own mental self-penetration and upon the degree of penetration of the object which I have achieved in my mind. This, in turn, will be based on the degree of detachment and silencing which I have attained. If mysticism was defined as *a thought thought through to its end,* we can also say that it is an *object seen unto its depth* and *a mind which has penetrated as far as its inner core.*

The object can be something *tangible,* immediately grasped by the senses:

* An image, an object seen.
* A sound directly heard.

It can have another, somewhat more interiorized form, as an *imagined* object.

The other senses can also be objects of our attention in the meditative process. However, the two senses just mentioned are more easily related to this process.

In both cases we find the same dynamics of *meditation,* whether they be directly felt (seen or heard) or imagined. I will deal with the slight variation of the imagined object further on.

For the time being I am going to limit myself briefly to what is directly seen since it is more common and important than what is heard.

1. Object seen

It is especially beneficial for beginners because it focuses the attention and it provides less mental dispersion.

> At the start of this path, the *tangible* sight is indispensable as the fertile womb of spiritual intelligence; if it were not so the latter would grieve over the lack of nourishment or it would degenerate into a rigid scheme. . . . The path to the very depth of the soul and to the encounter with God begins on the lowest tangible surface of imaginative contents. Meditation on an image is rooted in and justified by this fact.[74]

The outer and inner image represents an extremely important *affective* language. A healthy pedagogy aiming at modifying attitudes must necessarily use images. Modern man is not a *rational* but an *affective* man.

> Meditation on an image is entirely beset, submerged, surrounded and dominated by images. Man is often so engulfed in the world of images that it is only through images that he can be reached and influenced inwardly.[75]

The following preliminary exercise can help us learn to maintain our eyes on an object, but there must already be some degree of *concentration* to look fixedly at the object of meditation. Before meditation in front of a flower, a river, a photo or a painting, a person's portrait, etc., we must already be able to look at an object for a certain length of time. It is not absolutely necessary to look without moving the eyes, or without blinking, although it is certainly advisable. When the eyes move, so does the mind, or at least it tends to move; when the eyes are motionless, the thinking mind also tends to become motionless.

In Oriental yogi terminology, the following exercise destined to keep the eyes focused on an object *without motion*, without blinking, is called "trataka." It is called "concentration with eyes open."

- Keep gazing at an object, or a point, steadily, constantly, without blinking until tears come out or until you feel tired. You begin to feel a stinging sensation which you must resist and withstand until tears come. It usually follows quickly.
- When you feel tired or when you begin to cry, close your eyes and try inwardly to reproduce the object, to rebuild its image internally. Then, repeat the above. At first you will only sustain this gaze for a short time, one to three minutes at most. Gradually this time will increase and can even be one hour or more later.
- The trataka or fixed look of the eyes must be accompanied by the fixed look of the mind in total attention to the object.
- Your eyes may hurt at first. Simply avoid this by not going to the point of fatigue.
- This exercise gives a better mental control and fixation and, moreover, it strengthens the eyes and helps relax them.

As one looks fixedly one begins *to penetrate* the object. With time the object is seen within oneself. As we concentrate we are transformed into that on which we concentrate; we are transformed into what we gaze at daily. This, then, is the very process of meditation: by means of concentration, there occurs a unification between the meditator and the object. The eyes must not be tense at all; they must be relaxed, surrendered.

Sivananda applies meditation with trataka, a fixed look, to an image of Jesus and says:

> Place yourself before an image of the Lord Jesus in your favorite picture. Concentrate slowly, with your eyes open, on the image until tears stream down your cheeks.[76]

As a practical summary of this extremely important exercise, you may use the following points:

- Select any simple object.
- Look at it steadfastly without blinking.
- Your attention and mind must be totally centered on the object.
- Soon you will notice your eyes are stinging. You must resist it.
- Following the sting, tears will come and stream along your cheeks.
- Close your eyes and rest a moment. Then repeat the cycle.

You must look:

- Look without saying anything inwardly; simply look with interest. This is an attitude; it is not translated into words.
- Avoid tension in the eyes. Let them be relaxed.

This is already a form of meditation since there already occurs penetration of the mind and of the object looked at fixedly.

2. *Imagined Object*

The dynamics of meditation are exactly the same as in the previous case when one looks at the object, with this difference: that the object is reconstructed internally; it is imagined.

The preliminary preparation exercise for this meditation is not the trataka obviously, but another one called *visualization.*

- It consists of *reproducing* a concrete object internally in all its details as if you were seeing it.
- The visualization exercise will be well done when you are entirely tranquil, physically, affectively and mentally.

In reference to the object seen *interiorly* we must indicate the following:

- The imagined object corresponds to a greater degree of interiorization. It normally presupposes progress in a person's interiorization process. When you look fixedly at an image you reach the point when you feel the need to close your eyes.
- When you close your eyes, meaning to keep on meditating on the object, you must continue to see it, which implies the exercise of *visualization.*

Moreover, what usually happens when you close your eyes is a focusing on a certain *resonance* or interior echo which the object often produces, in which case you need not continue to look, although you may do so.

- Some people notice more distractions and more nervousness when they close their eyes. In that case, it is better to open them and to continue meditating on an external object until gradually silence and the need to close your eyes to delve in more deeply takes place. Many people concentrate better with their eyes open.

The intense nervousness or inner disruption which some feel often occurs in people whose subconscious is overburdened, filled with *desires, attachments* and anxieties.

How to Meditate on a Phrase

It is called *mantra* in the East. It can, in fact, be a phrase or only a word.

- "God is love"
- "Peace"

You can make up the mantra, phrase or word or take it from saints, poets, the Bible, famous men's words, etc.

Here are some mantras:

- "Unless a wheat grain dies, it remains only a single grain, but if it dies, it yields a rich harvest"
- "Whatever you do to the least of these, you do it to me"
- "Our Father"
- "In God we live and move and have our being"

- "Descend if you wish to ascend"
- "Man is the inner man"
- "God"
- "I can do everything in him who comforts me"
- "I will be your strength"
- "I loved you too late, O ancient beauty forever new, I loved you too late"

The phrase must be understood before beginning to meditate. Reading, study and therefore books can be helpful,

> so that, later, when we say the phrase it will automatically awaken affective and mental resonances in us.[77]

We call this preliminary study *enriching the phrase,* looking for its relations.

The phrase may appear under various forms and although I have already mentioned this earlier, I want to go into more detail.

1. Take the phrase as it appears and repeat it continuously:

- Having done the previous preparation.
- Totally attentive to the phrase.
- Repeating it slowly, very slowly.

Rather than concentrating on the specific words, concentrate on its meaning. As you simply repeat the phrase the suggested way, it begins to penetrate within and to yield its inner resonance.

> The constant repetition of a sentence containing the affirmation of a fundamental quality we wish to develop profoundly conditions the mind so as to facilitate the actualization of the quality or attitude which the phrase depicts.[78]

The following passage from a prayer diary clearly shows what I have just said:

> My mind remains lucid before the object of meditation—as time goes by *it seems as if the phrase were becoming more perceptive, something like what happens when you write with a pen; at first the strokes are light, and as you write the ink comes down and the strokes become clearer.* Almost at the end of the meditation, *I felt as if the phrase were filling up parts of my body:* head, arms, legs, eyes, etc.

This exercise alone is already a very interesting form of meditation although *very* frequently, at the beginning, people see it as a real *bore*, and totally meaningless.

> The constant repetition becomes automatic, gradually absorbing the habitual drifting of the mind so that when one voluntarily stops the phrase or mantra, there is authentic mental silence.[79]

You need not willfully stop the phrase. The constant repetition turns into silence, interiority, *inability to repeat* the phrase any longer. This takes place when you probe into deeper levels of the phrase and of the mind. It is a normal process of silencing which is attained after repeating the phrase for a long time; the following seems contradictory:

> I was bored with the repetition of the phrase, and if I do not repeat it, it seems I am doing nothing.

The phrase tends to vanish, leaving a vacuum which must be understood since it is close to contemplation as Blay notes:

> This single practice suffices, if it is carried out with due perseverance, to lead to the highest levels of spiritual fulfillment.[80]

Notice the inner state to which a nun's observations refer. As of the first day her whole meditation consisted of repeating her *mantra:* "God is love." After meditating for some time, repeating the phrase, she writes:

> All my meditations are characterized by deep recollection, total silence of all and my simply loving, gazing, praising and adoring. I have no need of words, or rather they disturb me.

2. However, the phrase can be *concretized*. Simultaneous with the repetition, the phrase can be projected in:

- Persons
- Objects, things
- Facts, events, situations

> While I repeated the phrase *God is love*, I concretized it mentally looking at a crucifix. My meditation was powerful (I would

like a clarification of this point). I ignore whether it is the work of the mind within meditation, or the result of the imagination, or both at the same time, but what an impact! I kept on repeating the phrase slowly while with the eyes of the soul I was seeing, looking at Jesus' wounds, one by one, with blood springing up from each one, his face crowned with thorns, his eyes without sight; his lips seemed to be telling me: *I love you.* I was looking at everything, pondering everything, and I was repeating more forcefully the phrase "God is love" made evident and witnessed in his gift of his divine Son to me. I concluded my meditation, and the image of Jesus crucified which I contemplated is following me, leaving a profound imprint within me.

We could have concretized love, the love God is and the love in which he holds us, in a *flower,* a *scene,* etc.

As the phrase is repeated one notices the gradual need of silence. If it is a phrase, either it is reduced to a word or it disappears at times, until repetition becomes impossible or annoying.

Something happens similar to what St. Augustine expresses:

In fact people who sing, whether it be at harvesting, grape harvest or any sort of intensive work, begin singing in words manifesting their joy; then, the joy pervading them becomes so intense that when they can no longer express it in words, they do without and they conclude in a simple jubilant sound.[81]

Despite the monotony, the seeming absurdity of foolishly repeating a phrase, possibly even meaningless at first, the first impression does not correspond to what takes place later. The phrase takes on power and depth. For that reason in India

the selection of the mantra is essential because when more subtle levels of the mind are reached, the thought becomes more powerful, like atomic power which is more powerful than chemical power.[82]

3. The third possible form of the phrase is abstract, without concretizing or repeating it.

Such phrases are *maxims, proverbs, abstract truths.*

- "In God we live and move and have our being"
- "The entire creation is groaning awaiting the revelation of the sons of God"
- "If God is with us, who can be against us?"

There are a thousand similar sentences. Here it is not a question of repeating the sentences but of *experiencing* them. It is done the following way as Mouni Sadhu teaches:

(a) First try to understand the meaning of the sentence.
(b) Then repeat it a few times only so that its clear contents register and settle in the mind. At this phase you proceed in the same fashion as when you repeat the phrase.
(c) Now stop repeating the verse and try to *extract* its inner content, as an idea without words. Know it, understand it, but the consciousness of it must not be veiled by the shadow of any words. Discard words and inner verbalization.

To clarify the meaning of this third phase, how to extract the inner content, to leave aside the words of the sentence, the external part, Mouni Sadhu gives this explanation:

> Imagine you are looking at a beautiful flower, recalling its shape, color, fragrance. Then close your eyes and, without thinking about the form of the flower, breathe in its sweet fragrance. At that moment you are conscious of the flower but without its visible appearance.[83]

Ways to Meditate Repeating a Phrase

This short section is a kind of appendix to meditation with a phrase.

The repetition of a phrase—*japam*—as I indicated earlier is a way to meditate. Now, I am going to show that the repetition of the phrase can be done along with two physiological and affective processes: relaxation and breathing.

1. Repetition along with relaxation:

Once you have relaxed, begin to repeat the sentence, again and again, in what appears to be a mechanical way without losing consciousness of it. This meditation is shown in the diagram below:

Each arrow shows the phrase. Meditation is the ordered, even, tranquil and conscious succession of the *same* phrase. Do not cling to it rapidly; return to it whenever you get distracted, but not later when silence occurs, and without losing consciousness, the phrase disappears.

2. Repetition along with breathing:

There are two possibilities: breathing can be simply lengthened without rhythm or it can be rhythmical.

- When breathing is only elongated, the phrase accompanies the inhalation and the exhalation as shown below:

inhale   exhale

In this context, *a phrase* can be a single word such as "God" as well as a phrase.

The word "God" or "peace," etc., is repeated, lengthening it during the time of the inhalation which must be slow and peaceful without efforts, and the same is done, lengthening the word when you exhale. If it is a phrase, it can be short; then you repeat it all as you inhale and as you exhale, for example: "I will always be strong."

If it is long, divide it in two parts. Say the first part as you breathe in and the second as you breathe out—for example: "If anyone loves me, my Father will love him/and we shall come to him and make our home within him." The slash indicates the possible break, the starting point for the exhalation.

- When breathing is rhythmical, each one must first determine his own rhythm by mentally counting the number of beats during the inhalation and exhalation. This rhythm is not left to chance, and it has specific characteristics which I am not explaining now but simply pointing out.

For most people a rather normal and adequate rhythm is 4-1-4. The inhalation lasts four beats; the air is kept in for one, coinciding with the apex between inhalation and exhalation. What is usually done is to count mentally: one, two, three, four—pause—one, two, three, four and so on. It can cause boredom. Besides, now we are meditating using a phrase. You choose a phrase with the adequate content which you want to penetrate. The phrase must contain as many syllables or groups of syllables as the rhythm established. For the previous rhythm 4-1-4 an adequate phrase could be: "Give me your peace" broken down into give-me-your-peace.

This is how it works: while you inhale, repeat the phrase, one syllable with each beat, which is easily done once you get the rhythm. In that case you need not count mentally. The phrase itself repeated rhythmically suffices. You may use the same phrase when you inhale and when you exhale; however the phrase may be long, which does not present any difficulty if you adjust its syllables to your rhythm.

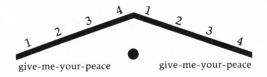

3. After practicing points 1 and 2 for ten minutes each, you now *stop all thoughts* and remain that way for ten minutes.

This does not deal with an *idea without words,* but an experience of the truth.

We simply pretend to lead the mind toward silence, self-penetration wherein nothing impairs the direct encounter with oneself, with things and with God. We achieve this inasmuch as it is feasible in this world.

How to Meditate on a Quality

We mean:

• Qualities such as humility, fortitude, simplicity, etc.
• Abstract realities such as life, sacrifice, love, etc.

We can consider a quality in its abstraction, but it is difficult to meditate directly on it. It is better to *give it a form* and allow the imagination to have a grasp which avoids dispersion and enables us to reach the heart of that quality.

As usual we must start with the understanding of that quality. Then it becomes concrete.

Example: Meditation on *God's love*

• Comprehend the meaning of God's love.
• concretize it in:
  • People
  • Things
  • Events

which express God's love. We may see a person, things or events from the point of view of meditation:

• God's love in Christ.
• A crucifix, work of God's love.
• The sea, a flower as a gift of God's love.
• A nurse tenderly caring for a patient exemplifies God's loving providence.

If we meditate on *humility* we can concretize it:

• In a humble person: seeing how he speaks, acts and moves. Look at him with *concentration, silently,* allowing yourself to be penetrated by the experience.
• In an object: a flower in the midst of grass or something somehow depicting humility.
• In an event, a scene: Jesus washing his disciples' feet.

The Happy Outcome of Meditation: Silence

All the previous objects of meditation are not possessed in *total* silence. There is always some intermediary between the meditator and the object: words, images or feelings. All these intermediary elements *distort* the genuine possession of the object.

Referring specifically to religious meditation, St. John of the Cross declares:

> Those who imagine God under any of these figures, as a great fire or light, thinking that what they see resembles God, are far away from him. Beginners need these reflections, forms and ways of meditation to attract and nourish their soul through the senses. . . . It must be a passing phase; they must not always remain there because in this fashion they would never reach the goal.[84]

> As the soul is coming closer to the spirit in its relationship with God it is progressively detached and freed from the way of the senses, namely discursive and imaginative meditation.[85]

The happy and logical outcome of meditation is the breaking away from all methods. In the end there are no ways.

> Therefore, on this road, beginning the way is to leave the road, or, better, it is to reach the goal; and to abandon one's way is to penetrate into what has no way, God, because the soul, having arrived at this stage, no longer has ways, or manners, nor does it lean on or cling to them. I refer to ways of understanding, liking or feeling, for this stage encompasses all ways.[86]

This state is the state of *silence.* There are, of course, degrees of silence, and the following example somewhat illustrates this aim of meditation, something about the final silent state. The example deals with the initial settling of silence; later it increased:

> As I had been repeating the usual phrase only for a few minutes, suddenly, without knowing how, I was submerged, as if dissolved in the contemplation of the Incarnate Word. All was silent: silence of the imagination, of the memory, without words, memories or even the remembrance of the principles I had studied concerning the great mystery of the Incarnate Word. There was only a look of love, admiration, amazement. It seemed that in today's meditation, with a single glance, I

was able to comprehend everything I had never grasped before. I conclude my meditation with great peace. I feel moved
to love God-Love with all my being. I feel the urgent need for
a total and full surrender as something which springs forth
very naturally after seeing what I saw.

The East calls what takes place, at the end of all meditations, pure
meditation, or meditation in silence.

I am concluding this chapter with some very useful advice from
St. John of the Cross for those who reach this silence:

This does not consist of working with the imagination, but in
the repose of the soul, letting it be in quietude and calm,
which is much more spiritual.[87]

Since they do not understand the mystery of this new state,
they imagine they are wasting time and doing nothing. Thus,
they do not let themselves be quiet; they keep on reasoning
and discoursing.[88]

Many spiritual people err after having striven to reach God
through images, forms and meditations adequate for beginners, when God wants to draw them into more spiritual, inner
and invisible heights.... They do not stop, they do not
dare.[89]

They must be told to learn to be in God in that quietude attentively and in loving awareness.[90]

7 THE EFFECTS OF MEDITATION

- *Total Reconstruction*
- *Strength and Direction of the Mind*
- *Degree of Depth of the Modifications*
- *Mental Integration*
- *Meditation and the Nervous System*
- *Meditation and Physical Changes*
- *Meditation and Affective Changes*
- *The Mind Creates New and More Stable Meanings*
- *A More Profound Way of "Being" Takes Place:*
  1. Being Beyond Time and Space
  2. Being in Silence
- *Meditation Improves Interpersonal Relationships*
- *Purer Spirituality and Closeness to God*

Meditation itself is not a religious act. It is simply a technique of mental penetration, although meditation applied to the in-depth probing of the religious dimension of everyone is of fundamental concern, and it is under that perspective that I consider it here. When meditation becomes a search for God through the search of and encounter with oneself, its effects are of two kinds:

- Some caused by the gradual penetration into a person's various levels. These results can be observed and noticed up to a point, as results of the work or as symptoms of a deeper work of inner growth.
- Others are produced by God's presence in the meditator's life. Grace is an authentic event but not directly noticeable. One neither directly observes it nor is it logically inferred from anything. One simply *believes* in the faithfulness of God who gives himself to the open person.

In this latter case the symptoms are those of someone becoming a person, observing phenomena vouching for his human growth. They are a guarantee of openness to God; therefore they invite us to believe that God's presence will follow a person's growth simply because God is faithful.

Even if the meditator does not center his meditation on God, he still grows as a person, more open to the discovery of the religious dimension. Consequently, all that involves becoming more of a person is, in the final analysis, a *religious event.*

Total Reconstruction

Meditation really generates a total personal reconstruction.

• The integration of the nervous system and muscular levels.
• The integration of the emotional life.
• The integration of the mind.

As a daily surprise, a previous unknown and unexpressed personality *begins to appear.* The will is also different, not the will *striving* to move in a specific direction, but simply *willing.* Meditation assumes a personal renewal for oneself and for others. Nothing occurring in meditation is exclusive; all I am or can be occurs not only to the meditator, since relationships, co-existence and presence are inevitable. One's individuality and its projection toward God and neighbor are restructured.

The first sign of this reconstruction is an overwhelming feeling of *unity:*

The creation of the personality does not dwell in physical expressions but in the unification of the mind.[91]

Thought is the guiding factor in this renewal. In India, there is a principle which is repeated ad nauseam:

One of the great laws of nature is that a man becomes what he thinks. Think you are a Brahman, and you will become a Brahman.[92]

This thought marks the direction of a person's transformation. This is why the selection of the object of meditation is of the utmost importance. It will mark the direction of the look though not the act of seeing. The mind provides the strength needed to continue in the direction of the thought.

Strength and Direction of the Mind

We often notice either in our lives or in other people's lives that things occur only because we wish them, or because we think intensely about them, or because we fear them. This has nothing to do with what some may immediately think of the present exposition. Suggestions are lies, and their authors are liars: *I imagine I am handsome and I am; if I am fat I think I am going to get thin and I get thin.* Apart from these fictions, there are many things which enable us to assert that the mind has a power of projection which can be negative or positive. Psychosomatic medicine studies the mind's negative projection on the patient's body. Many diseases are known to have a mental or psychic origin.

Blay states:

> If we seek the profound explanation of the enormous effectiveness of meditation, first of all we need to understand this principle well: *all that we are objectively and subjectively is only a product of the mind.*[93]

Within our theist and Christian context, we claim to proceed from God, to be a creation of God's mind and to be rooted in Christ, reborn with *his new spirit.* At the same time the human mind, made in the image and likeness of God, keeps on projecting itself on everything.

- Giving form or *forming* the environment in which it projects itself. The environment, things, reflect the state of the human mind.
- Changing forms or *reforming* the physical and mental environment. This function of the human mind is called *alloplasia* or the capacity to give plasticity to all that surrounds a person. We must, however, point out that what surrounds a person does not end with what can be seen or touched. The mind's range goes much further, and the possibility of modifying things goes way beyond what we know now.
- Forming itself or *conforming,* according to which one can *adapt* from oneself when one cannot do so from the things one uses, if at some point one cannot use them. We call this capacity for self-modification, *autoplasia.* One can modify one's body, affectivity and mind.

Levels of Depth of These Modifications

In everyone, there are mental levels determining the degree of influence on the environment and on oneself.

I do not intend to describe the subconscious or conscious so common to all psychological treatises. I simply want to state that a strong, influential and also positive person (in the previously mentioned areas) is not the result of a conscious or subconscious mind but of an *integration* of all the mental aspects, of everyone's unique mind. For that reason we read in a Tibetan work:

If someone asks you what is the nature of meditation, answer that it is the secret of being able to give up all imaginative thoughts with the seeds which bring them forth.[94]

Meditation, the activity of a mind which probes deep within itself, is the result of the convergence of the thinking mind and of the mind from which the thought proceeds, the hidden mind where what we call *seeds* (attitudes and accumulated experiences) are concealed. In the cited passage, we observe something about which I will speak later: the integration must be achieved by letting go of thoughts and letting go of the seeds, namely, in *silence.*

There exists a mind vivifying all aspects of life. There is a mind wherein converge what in the Orient is called physical consciousness, affective consciousness and intellectual consciousness. This does not mean that all the aspects of the mind and consciousness are exhausted. This mind to which all converges is the mind which we want to discover. In it is rooted the total effectiveness of meditation.

Since the mind is the meeting point of impressions proceeding from all levels of the personality, a kind of center directing behavior in all its aspects, it must evidently be related in its various degrees of depth with every single level, performing a specific function with each one.[95]

This means that the mind is connected with everything drawing strength from it: the body, affectivity and the mind itself. It means that the mind can penetrate itself in depth and it does so in meditation. Consequently what is corporal, affective and mental is penetrated in depth in meditation.

This is why one cannot probe in depth in meditation without a simultaneous integration of the mind and without a behavior reflecting this integration. Since behavior is always manifested through the nervous system, it must also become integrated as the mind is gradually unified in meditation.

Mental Integration

I referred to the progressive unification of the mental aspects when I dealt with the preparation for meditation.

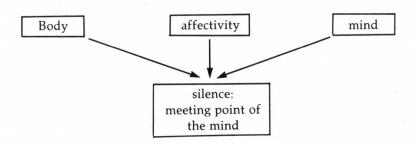

The body, the affectivity and what we call mind gain in depth as they move toward this central point called silence where they meet.

Then, silence is physical silence obtained through relaxation; it is affective silence reached through pacification, and it is silence of mental contents, thoughts, images, etc., obtained through mental silence.

To the degree that unification is taking place, meditation becomes more effective. It is understandable that an idea introduced in a unified mind:

• is always introduced in the in-depth mind.
• immediately affects a person's physical life.
• modifies the affectivity.

There, at the point of convergence of practically everything, there is only one reality: consciousness, lucidity in total silence. Everything is simultaneously body, affectivity and mind.

When someone is unified in this way, one immediately reaches the depth of whatever is suggested, or, better still, what is suggested penetrates within as far as one's inner silence permits. The suggestion of an idea, a thought in such a state, is what Rammurti Mishra calls *suggestion,* which has nothing in common with the popular understanding of auto-suggestion. Rammurti's suggestion is meditation itself.

Notice that the essence of this mental unification is *concentration* which can also be negative. So, someone who totally concentrates on a negative idea has a mind unified in that direction.

What is suggested while in that state will have immediate effects:

> It is a well-known fact that through suggestion there can be a paralysis or its cure, burns or insensitivity to burns, and not only insensitivity in the case of superficial burns, but even the absence of blood. In short, extraordinary results can be attained. Normal physiological laws are not suppressed but they are profoundly altered. It appears as if physiology were a prolongation of the mind.[96]

This indicates that the effects of a unified mind will go beyond the mind itself, reaching our physiology. One can verify how meditation changes physiological habits and raises the general state of well-being in which physiology plays an important role.

In summary, to conclude this section, let me stress that from the unified, silent, in-depth mind, a person's conscious or subconscious mental substance can be modified, and so too the affective nature and consequently the life-style and the physiological limitations can be modified and even strongly altered as the following experience indicates:

> Lord, I believe; help my faith. I relaxed totally and quickly— my mind was increasingly clear. At first my head was pounding with the rhythm of each word. Little by little I entered into profound silence—total void, as if I were hanging over a dark and hollow well. My mind remained lucid before the object of my meditation. As time goes by, *it seems as if the phrase were becoming more perceptive. . . . Almost at the end of meditation, I felt as if the phrase were filling up parts of my body:* head, arms, legs, eyes, etc.
>
> *(Prayer diary of a nun)*

In this quotation, you notice the presence of silence where the mental unification previously described occurs. At that moment the phrase representing the mental aspect is unified with the body, arms, legs, etc. It is a beautiful example of good work.

I sleep only six hours and I do not feel tired (just a little at night). Before I got tired with more sleep. The morning meditation awakens me mentally (I am referring to the purely physical aspect).

(Prayer diary of a youth)

Meditation and the Nervous System

In fact, what we call *nerves* improves. One who is *a bundle of nerves* improves considerably. These sayings, though accurate, are a naive, common way of speaking, but deep down lies a very interesting question, namely, the way one's nervous system is affected by meditation. At the same time, it is true also that the gradual improvement of one's nervous system permits a more profound meditation.

One's whole structure heads toward increasing integration at higher levels, and the nervous system works *in connection with* all of one's layers:

- connecting the various mental aspects: physical, affective and conscious mind;
- connecting with one's natural dimensions: religious, all that involves one's living with others in a specific environment.

To improve along all these lines is the best proof of the degree of unification of the nervous system.

The nervous system allows greater depths of consciousness. From a more unified nervous system emerges a more subtle state of consciousness, since consciousness, the mind, functions through the nervous system. Maharishi Mahesh even speaks of a physiological method of union with God. Taken out of context, this seems absurd, but in fact it is not. Indeed, we know that the state of mind of a fulfilled person, a holy person, has ramifications in the nervous system. The unity within a person leads us to deduce that if we can *unify the nervous system,* the state of consciousness characteristic of a fulfilled person will automatically change. I am saying "state of consciousness" which does not mean having the same ideas nor the same explanations for such a state. Specifically, Christian revelation introduces ideas and affirmations non-existent among people who are outside the explicit Christian revelation, although they may be holy: their explanation of the same experience will be different.

Thus the nervous system begins to develop and renew itself through meditation and the positive experiences it brings about.

When a person returns to daily life after the moments devoted to meditation, he returns more rested, with a greater serenity pervading all he does or says. One's senses are sharper and the level of muscular tension is at its best.

Although I do not wish to go into more detail or explanations about the nervous system and spirituality, past experiences attest to the fact that spirituality improves the nerves. The reverse is also true: disturbed nerves indicate a lack of integration of the nervous system, lack of unity of consciousness or a consciousness altered by negative experiences, basically insufficient spiritual life or insufficient stability.

In the following section, I am presenting testimonies and experiences of people I have introduced to meditation and who continue to practice regularly. I discard all those whose experience has been passing or not in depth because of a lack of continuity and regular practice.

I am presenting the experiences according to the area to which they belong. In this manner, the experience or phenomenon can be identified within the phases of development and according to the levels of depth previously mentioned.

These are only a few of the many examples occurring in the meditation process and among the many which I have encountered in my work. They relate to fundamental characteristics of personal changes and to the way we understand perfection in the West.

Meditation and Physical Changes

At the silent point where the mind, affectivity and body converge, any idea or object of meditation must have a corporal effect, and this is natural. First you notice a general feeling of newness, of well-being; you feel less tired and more rested.

On the other hand, meditation presupposes a gradually deeper relaxation which alters the muscular tone, destroying tensions and the ensuing fatigue; metabolism is also altered and a better corporal functioning sets in at all levels. The nervous system is revived, the central system as well as the autonomous or neuro-vegetative system which controls metabolism and the vegetative function. Psychological sciences have shown an important fact that people become what they think, because their thoughts shape them.

The influence of thought reaches the body, and physically too people become what they think as thoughts fashion their bodies; the bodily image is the external image which the inner person, or the person in depth offers to the world.

Meditation involves precisely that extraordinary power to shape not only internally but also externally. When one meditates on something, in a continuous way, day after day, hour after hour, little by little, one tends to transform oneself into what occupies one's mind.[97]

We commonly say that the face is the mirror of the soul. This comes from the observation of daily experience although it is based on a much broader and entirely scientific principle. Indeed, the whole body is the mirror of the soul, of a person's mind, and so the agitation of the mind transmits itself to the body. However, the face—this mirror of the interpersonal experience—is more affected, so that different mental states can be read on a person's face.

The face of someone who meditates assiduously is changing, acquiring a look of *non-tension,* of peace and serenity which can be striking though not frightening. Rather, it is reassuring because it radiates friendship, closeness and transparence. Far from being an enigmatic face concealing expression, it is the face of someone expressing a superior and mysterious vision of the world.

Meditation and Affective Changes

A brief definition of affectivity could be: "The quality of a person in his totality, created by the repercussion in the whole organism of the meanings which the mind attributes to persons, situations or things."

The meditator produces a slow but effective *liberation* from everything. As freedom increases, affectivity decreases, or rather it is not affectivity which is destroyed but the uncontrolled impact of things on people. This lack of control would give rise to an *uncontrolled* affectivity or an affectivity controlled *from the outside* because things predominate. Meditation engenders control. The freely chosen object of meditation imposes its rhythm to everything. Everything begins to acquire the look of what I meditate on. Controlled affectivity through meditation is an affectivity unified by the object of meditation. Such a unified affectivity is quite distinct in its manifestation and degree from that which is determined by the objects which dominate a person. As a manifestation it is entirely positive; as to its degree, it is not intermittent but gradually more intensive although more serene in its expressions.

I want to forestall a possible difficulty or objection: since meditation is a technique, it can be used for evil. This is true to a degree. Since it is a growing process of unity in the person, it will eliminate anxiety, tension, remorse. Someone who works evil, who is totally directed toward evil, is doing meditation, but it is an imposed meditation, a pseudo-meditation because freedom is lacking. The results will, of course, be very different.

Pacification is almost a common fact as it occurs frequently. You begin to notice degrees of serenity, of tranquility such as the following testimonies describe:

> This state of peace which I reach during meditation is lasting throughout the day. Things affect me less, almost not at all today. Things which elated me or depressed me before have no hold on me.

> Today I have had a great deal of peace, a peace which fills me from head to toe. I wish that this morning meditation would continue throughout every minute of the day as today.

> During the month, I have kept this inner equilibrium throughout the day, although I have lost it on some occasions.

> I realize that something unusual is happening in me, in my daily life. My whole being is pacified; an inner and serene joy overwhelms me; things have no power over me. I overlook them and walk on in peace.

> Normally during the day I am more tranquil and therefore I have better control of the situation.

It often happens that, to people looking *without intelligence,* at first sight one may show characteristics akin to introversion, apathy, absence, indifference:

> It seems that my feelings of sympathy or antipathy diminish, or I cannot discern them.

This same person said earlier that her love was expanding and that she loved everyone *without exception.* But then, she believes she is indifferent or apathetic. She simply does not know how to discern.

> Over the past few days, I experienced spiritual stability throughout the day. At work, I have been told I was sad, but it is not so. I know it was spiritual calmness.

As a person penetrates into his own mind, he begins to enter into a situation created during his meditation, a state of silence and peace.

Liberation occurs right from the beginning, imperceptibly at first, but firmly. This is seen as a certain absence from things and even from interpersonal experience by common people, whereas it simply marks a change in the way of relating, and what seems like sleep is a state of inner peace.

All of this belongs to the realm of the paradoxical best suited to express what is inexpressible, to say what is unspeakable as the following verses well suggest:

Sleep sleeps in us
while we are awake,
and we fall asleep
when sleep awakens.[98]

There is an interiority which does not come forth when one is ruled and affected by external things, but it emerges when one becomes at peace, freeing oneself from what is external.

Within the context of pacification we observe the disappearance of all the forms of lack of peace:

- Aggressiveness, which is a form of destroying others, an ineffective form of self-assertion. Some have reached a stage where they declare they *cannot get angry.* This, however, does not decrease the *fighting spirit* which is needed in the daily struggle; instead it increases it precisely because fear disappears.
- Fear, apprehensions stemming from an inadequate way of living: isolated, different, opposed to others. It is a way *to live without love,* destroying our unity as we assert, *with little intelligence,* our individual differences. When we see ourselves as being different, easily translated by *opposed,* we live defensively. This attitude generates fear, apprehension and aggressiveness.

God's peace will build upon this peace, which is not only lack of aggressiveness and fear, but inner harmony and control. Once again, grace builds on nature. The absence of aggressiveness and fear opens the way to human maturity, just as God's love excludes fear. This new peace, God's peace and man's peace, are no longer two; they are one.

And that peace of God, which is much greater than we can understand, will guard your hearts and your thoughts in Christ Jesus.[99]

The following quotation concluding this section is a valuable testimony for meditation-prayer where anxieties and fears gradually disappear:

> I surrendered, willing to accept all moral or physical sufferings that the Father in his love should prepare for me so that priests may be holy and religious life may be renewed along the lines of the Council. I achieved this with great peace, inner joy, in an unexplainable experience of filial surrender, fearing *nothing,* remaining in God's hands.
>
> (*Prayer diary of a nun*)

Peace is both the result and the best sign that a different, positive way of seeing oneself is beginning to be a reality. It is also the result of meditation. On the other hand, the absence of fear is not a negative state; it is a state of *harmony* stemming from a sense of inner *oneness* with everything; it is the consciousness of oneness, of love.

The Mind Creates New and More Stable Meanings

A *mind change* is only possible when one meditates. In meditation attitudes are restructured, especially one's character which is a *generalized attitude.*

Character represents:

- A way of seeing oneself.
- A way of seeing one's relations with the world.
- A way of seeing a specific relation with the world: relationship with others.

As it progresses, meditation leaves us with its effective imprint in terms of character:

> One of the signs of progress along the way is the disappearance of *yesterday's me* as we look at it with today's perspective. This is the best proof of the profound changes taking place in me.[100]

I have many testimonies along these lines too. Many people who assiduously practice the meditation I have taught them notice with surprise that they are changing; what they could not dream of before is occurring; what they longed for is now being achieved.

Not very long ago, a few short months, I was an untamable little colt. July 16 [the first day of the spiritual exercises] became a landmark in all my life and for my whole life. What radical changes in the depth of my being, I do not know myself.

At times, everything seems irrelevant or mere routine; but looking in depth, I think I am getting rid of something; I feel a little freer as if peeling off onion skins and I have removed one.

I lost my self-image. It was not real. I have the impression I worked a long time at identifying myself with the positive aspect of things, but I remained caught up in them.

I confess that I feel strange, new. I compare myself with yesterday's X [she inserts her name] and I see less and less in common.

This new self-perception appears as a liberation:

This meditation-prayer has freed me from many things beginning with liberation from myself, from this self, this deeply-rooted center of all in spite of my continuous struggles and efforts to control myself. I found this great treasure of real prayer and meditation so late! And so, I ardently wish many people might discover it and enjoy its benefits.

I repeat that I feel I am floating somewhere and that the external world is getting further away from me, or vice versa (I from it). It is there and I find myself more outside of it, freer though I am still in it.

I seemed to be further away from things, in a vacuum, but I am at ease.

As one acquires freedom, when the *predominance* of things decreases, the person begins to find himself. This is the risk and the great discovery of freedom: self-encounter beyond all the masks, and so a more inner and authentic self-perception is born:

> I also discover my inner self with great clarity. Before, I managed to see and discover my faults after tremendous efforts, and even then many details escaped me. Now, I notice quickly whatever prevents my progress toward sanctity. Each meditation becomes a light, an awakening, a warning.

> I usually feel small, bad when I go to prayer, lacking that *something* (not all the time, but very frequently).

> It seems that I am losing my self-image; it was too good and unreal. I see many ugly things in me which I never noticed before.

When interiority appears and dominates life, life becomes simple. Interiority is necessarily simple and uncomplicated if it is authentic because the spirit manifesting itself is simple and uncomplicated. Complication is the obstacle raised between the spirit and things which prevents us from seeing the inside and the outside and which does not allow us to see that the inside and the outside are not such different things; they have continuity. When interiority becomes clear, so does the environment.

> I look at everything with new eyes: a flower, a tree, a mountain, a scene, a river, the serenity of the blue sky. All the beauty of nature speaks another language, much more eloquent ever since I started to meditate and I tried to assimilate and penetrate into the phrase: God is love.
>
> (*Prayer diary of a nun*)

Everything is taking on new meanings which is one of the great values of meditation.

> I have realized that the meaning of our actions is much more fundamental than the actions themselves. Meditation gives meaning. Without it, I feel I would not know how to live my religion.

Daily life as a whole acquires a new meaning coming from meditation. The following quotation shows its projection in the life of liturgical prayer and personal devotions:

> With this technique of meditation-prayer I am achieving my desire *to unify* my spiritual life by leaps and bounds. In the liturgical hours while I recite the psalms, in every word I seem to see my meditation phrase, "God is love" reflected; in all of them I find the same meaning; affection spontaneously springs forth from within enriching community prayer. The same thing happens when I reflect on the Word of God either on my own or during Holy Mass. Since I know how to concentrate to meditate, it turns out that I discover the meaning of what the Lord wants to tell me in his Word, almost by intuition. I noticed it on very rare occasions before, after extraordinary efforts to concentrate and to empty myself, and now it surrounds me powerfully, making demands of me and exhorting me. My visits to the Blessed Sacrament are also different from those of previous times: spontaneous, loving; a look which says it all, a sense of adoration coming from within rather than the outcome of feelings aroused with great effort.
>
> *(Prayer diary of a nun)*

A More Profound Way of "Being" Takes Place

As one progresses in meditation, a new way of being is being born. It is a being in silence in which the *normal* conditioning of the *normal* person, e.g., time and space, is overcome. It is a being which does not admit the questions "Where are you?" or "When will you be in?" but closer to the question "How are you?" because it certainly expresses an inner state, as when one says "I feel well," for it is only when time is transcended that truth ceases to be abstract.

Silence, or suppressing words, is closely related to time and space. The experience of the disappearance of time and space along with the appearance of silence shapes this new way of being, transcending theory and becoming the daily experience of meditators.

1. Being beyond time and space

The mind is a unique reality in all men, though its development may vary and the explanations of the mental phenomena may also vary. All inner people notice what mystics proclaim: mental in-depth penetration leaves aside time and space. Psychology itself points out that there exists the time measured by the clock and the time considered by a person or psychological time. The first is unvaried, but the second, depending upon a person's inner state, varies; thus five minutes may seem like hours and hours may seem like seconds. Meditation tends to overcome time because it can control it and because it knows that what is eternal is beyond time. Time represents a construction of the mind and reflects the mind's inner state, and the same is true of space.

> The more we analyze time and space, the more they become little more than an idea. Time is the movement of the mind. The mind can only think in terms of *before, now* and *after* or past, present and future. According to yoga philosophy, *reality* is beyond time and space.[101]

St. John of the Cross gives his version within our Christian context. He refers to the loss of time which always implies loss of space. I do not pretend to enter into philosophical digressions, irrelevant at this point, but simply to come to a verification provided by the experience that it happens in this fashion. This is what St. John of the Cross says about contemplation:

> The purity and simplicity of this infused knowledge is the cause of this ecstasy. This knowledge invades the soul leaving it simple, pure and free from all ideas and forms of the senses and memory, and therefore it leaves it in oblivion and unaware of time. Although this prayer may last a long time, it seems very brief because the soul has been united in pure intelligence which is outside of time.[102]

The above quotation shows the overcoming of time as the outcome of the contemplative state, not of meditation. When St. John of the Cross speaks of meditation, he refers to the discursive kind, whereas I refer to meditation in the sense of penetration of one's mind. This penetration continues in contemplation, and in that sense contemplation is also meditation.

> During meditation you have no concept of time; no sound, no idea of what surrounds you reaches you.[103]

This, obviously, does not happen so completely at the beginning. There is a gradual absence; there is a gradually weaker connection with the environment which does not suddenly disappear. The progressive disappearance of time and space will be the very sign of self-penetration in depth. This very openness to the inner self allows the absence of all that comes through time and space without falling asleep. If a person leaves time and space without having built this new way, he inevitably falls asleep.

The following experiences only aim at showing how a mind going toward greater depth modifies what we believe to be so real and important. For the moment I am not dealing with the degree of an in-depth penetration, but there are many different degrees and some of them are very profound.

Between preparation in the chapel and meditation in my room . . . I have spent two hours which seemed a very short time.

I did not notice I was breathing. There came a moment so intense that I did not know if I was sitting or in the air, if I had arms and legs. Before such an occurrence and whenever it happens, *I have the impression of being asleep.* (How does one distinguish?)

My mind was so firm, absorbed, engrossed, I was not saying anything and yet my mind was very active; the notion of time, place, space, people, everything was concealed then. I thought I was alone in the chapel, and yet when I concluded my meditation, I saw a sister meditating next to me.

I was in deep concentration without noticing where I was, in what posture, the time spent—which seemed short, though it was rather long.

2. Being in silence

Silence is the first and the last dimension of being human. The strongest and most authentic forms of human expression emerge from a person's silence, and one always returns to silence when wanting to discover the meaning of all human expressions. The best disposition for grasping everything *as it is,* without distortions, is silence. It is all the more so when dealing with encountering God; the experience will necessarily be more genuine when it occurs in the greatest silence. For that reason St. John of the Cross warns:

Thus it is better to learn to bring the faculties to silence and quietude, that God may speak.[104]

Silence cannot be reduced to external silence, meaning the absence of noises, nor to being quiet. The silence in which *one is* is silence of the *whole person*. Relaxation, pacification and the absence of thought shape this silence, or, rather, they shape the silent person.

Lack of silence means muscular and nervous tension in the body, agitation in the affectivity, and what we might call *inner chatter* or verbalization in the mind. In fact, this inner chatter is at the root of the previous states of lack of silence and its cessation will give peace and calm to the body and the mind.

To verbalize is *to name* things, persons, situations. The silenced mind stops naming. It does not perceive things through the names it has given them, but directly, without naming them. For Westerners whose education is rooted more in words and formulas than in realities, this proves very difficult. Yet, this tendency to name must be stopped because the closeness which man may attain on his way to God will never be reached through our ideas of God, but only through our silence before God. Ideas only translate what I think of God; silence allows God to reveal himself, without distortions, more purely. Silence is a normal outcome of meditation. At first, silence can be intermittent, fluctuating or even ambiguous, similar to the border zone between alert silence and the silence of one who falls asleep, but this is gradually overcome, until one arrives at silence which is alertness and consciousness.

I remained inwardly silent. I was not repeating the phrase, but I was not distracted nor was I feeling anything. Perhaps I fell asleep. I do not know.

There came a moment so intense that I did not know if I was sitting or in the air, if I had arms and legs. Before such an occurrence and whenever it happens, *I have the impression of being asleep.* (How does one distinguish?)

My head seemed to get bigger, as if inflated, while inside it seemed that everything was going round and round, creating a vacuum in the center of my brain, leaving it free, something like the clothes you put in an automatic dryer which, while it spins very fast, creates a vacuum in the center, and the clothes cling to the sides, all being accompanied by rhythmic beats. Suddenly there came great silence within (the dryer stopped). . . . I was repeating the phrases slowly, calmly and immersed in profound silence.

I felt freer than ever from everything which helped me concentrate more on my meditation. Over half an hour passed, *I was repeating the phrase more slowly, until finally I remained hanging on to a single word, "God," lengthened, pondered, tasted.* I did not know what was happening but *it seemed as if I were falling within, in the depth of a great mystery never completely revealed, with always more to discover. When only the word "God" remained in me, it seemed that all that could be thought, said, discovered about him were concentrated there.* Then, usually, I say nothing, I only look.

As a summary of what has been said in the last two sections, the following quotation shows an advanced stage of meditation and also the *being in silence, beyond time and space.*

I fell on my knees oblivious of the uncomfortable posture. I have no idea how long I remained that way, absorbed, firm, motionless. I ignore what I said, if in fact I said anything. I was simply there, loving, gazing at the Lord, wishing to penetrate into his heart, to be there, to find solace in him and to be his Bethany, that home where he found love, rest, refreshment. I cannot say if I spent one hour or more. I did not notice the hour when I began, and when I finally had to end, I realized it was very late.

The beginnings are obviously not like that. There are different rhythms of work and growth. Growth can take place without our knowing when or to what degree; such a growth is God's doing. Thus, to work efficiently, we need faith in God along with regular serious work. To rest in God is also part of silence, since one does not cease to talk until one surrenders one's cares to God.

Meditation Improves Interpersonal Relationships

When one meditates one becomes more peaceful, which is immediately reflected in relationships, since a pacified person *does not defend himself* against anyone. A pacified person keeps open the channels of communication with the world and with people. What has been previously said about the affective repercussions of meditation finds its application here.

To be open is a new attitude needed for interpersonal relationships. Every attitude has a double reference and a double influence:

- Influence on the stimuli coming from within (memories, images, etc.) and from the outside. From the incoming stimuli we only perceive those to which our attitude has sensitized us, and they are in the same line as daily meditation. Consequently when we meditate, we begin to reorganize the world of things and people in the way in which they influence us. This way of influencing us determines the other dimension of an attitude.
- One's reaction and behavior. It is normal that one's reaction, reflecting one's thought and expression of an inner attitude, should stimulate others who react according to my behavior.

We call this action and reaction, this interchange between people, interaction which is the expression of coexistence. Its origin is in one's attitude, in one's thoughts. Thinking, therefore, involves a great responsibility because, as Sivananda states, a thought is similar to a boomerang returning to the person who threw it. This is fulfilled in the Gospel: "The amount you measure out is the amount you will be given," which need not only apply to God's judgment but to interpersonal relationship.

In meditation, the thoughts chosen are always positive and filled with religious content, although the latter may be lacking, especially in psychological meditation aiming at character changes and based on merely psychological motivation. As one focuses on positive thinking, negative thoughts withdraw and interpersonal relationships improve. However, this is not the only cause of improvement in relationships emerging from meditation. In pacification, previously mentioned, with the destruction of a person's physical and emotional tensions, his capacity for aggressiveness, fear, discontent and anxiety is reduced. In fact, the person who meditates develops a more profound and less exclusive love for people. One need not work directly with charity for this phenomenon to occur. When the degree of tensions is lowered, then the goodness that man is appears and God's goodness manifests itself through the person open to God. I am giving some examples of people who have experienced this growth with its internal and external orientation without any knowledge of the explanation above. The classification is inadequate since other people are loved more and more and they are more within. The separation between you and me, between outside and inside, is overcome and destroyed. Everything is becoming one which shows that the process of *love* encompasses everything, making it one. Here are some testimonies:

I notice that I love people without exclusiveness.

I help everybody, plugging holes wherever they may be; available, obliging as I have never been. There is a force in me which moves me like a spring before the slightest hint of other people's needs. I can go out of my way for others before they have to sacrifice or give up anything, yet all of this without premeditation. There is no room for it since someone in me quickly impels me to help, to lend a hand whenever necessary.

I am noticing how my former uncontrolled need for affection is vanishing so rapidly that I do not understand. I am no longer dependent upon what people will say or wish. I am more at ease with oblivion than in my anxious struggle to obtain great success, great things which seem more and more insignificant.

The above shows greater freedom and at the same time a new attitude in relationships which are peaceful instead of competitive and distressing. To be with people becomes more pleasant.

I find myself more flexible, ready, solicitous with others' needs, little details without being noticed or seen. I simply anticipate their needs.

I have realized that love is the goal of man's life, the goal of meditation, a unique love encompassing God and men, in one single reality. I realize that we are all important, and that we are all One. Throughout the day when I remember, I become conscious of *this* and I really marvel; it leads me to other people.

My experience in meditation simply causes me to be with God all the time. His presence follows me, accompanies and surrounds me. It is normal for me to spend the day in a constant being with him, wherever I may be, and I am also so sensitized to his presence in others that I am not indifferent to anyone; my hand is offered to everyone; I am ready to please, understand everyone. All of this happens gently, simply, without a need to search or prepare for it.

I came out of meditation transformed (a little, not deeply). I was rushing to love the whole world, knowing that each human being contains a mystery worthy of love.

Purer Spirituality and Closeness to God

As I have already indicated, meditation is a technique of penetration within one's mind. It is a mental technique which can be applied to different areas, providing different types of meditation:

- psychological meditation
- philosophical meditation
- religious meditation

We are naturally dealing with religious meditation in which, as I have suggested, one's character is greatly improved, but, above all, spirituality is improved, e.g., one's relationship with God and the manner in which one lives it. I conclude this chapter (without more comments) with testimonies concerning *some effects of meditation.*

I continued to meditate and *as I concentrated, I had the tangible feeling of Jesus' presence in our midst. It seemed that if I opened my eyes, I could easily see him sitting here, accompanying us with his presence. The impact of this experience was very great; then I concluded my meditation; I entered into prayer and reflection whose effects I still feel today, so many days afterward.*

I really probed in depth. I felt very close to him, especially at the end of the twenty minutes when I left the church.

It was good to be in God's presence. I am more used to it now. I do not know the extent of God's holiness nor the extent of my wickedness, but it seems to me that the hope that my filiation will one day reach its fulfillment is increasing in me.

Something unusual must have happened to me because at dawn I realized that, following a very peaceful night, I woke up dialoguing with God spontaneously, lovingly for half an hour until getting up time.

I tried to stay with *God*. I was comfortable. I felt he was close.

I only feel like being in the chapel; rather, it feels like I am taking the chapel with me though I am not in it. I understand God. I do not know how this can happen, because I do not know if it is so, and I am afraid to say it for fear I am not making myself clear. I say I do not know how this can happen because, until recently, people spoke to me about him and I used to laugh; perhaps my inability to comprehend kept me away, and yet now it is that tremendous force which somehow leads me to him.

When the half hour rang, I entered again into depth with the impression that God, with a capital "G," was so close to me, I could almost feel his breath. Within my mind, a great light; in such circumstances I cannot repeat the phrase. I remain bewildered.

I was really concentrating on the phrase "God-Love." My whole body felt warm, especially my hands, and as if a stream of blood were rising through my throat, and yet the church was not very warm. I had the feeling (somewhat vague) that God was not very far.

I concentrated on the word "God." For a while I felt immersed in him. I was happy, and the good part of it is that this feeling stayed with me the whole day.

I have probed myself in depth. I felt there was something more with me. I have spoken about this something on other occasions. I came out happy, with a happiness which lasted until I went to bed.

I have not specified the state of each person, including their declarations into one quotation. Religious, students, young men and women have written them.

8

HOW CAN WE KNOW IF WE MEDITATE WELL?

- *The Adventure of Those Who Meditate*
- *Degrees of Depth in Meditation*
- *Stages in the change of Character Through Meditation*
  1. Stage of the Initial Impact
  2. Stage of the Change in Depth
     (a) Assimilation period
     (b) Anxiety connected with growth
  3. Stage of Greater Integration and Mental Stability
- *Signs of Progress in the Second Phase*
- *Signs of Progress in the Third Phase*

The Adventure of Those Who Meditate

I dedicate this chapter to those who have begun to meditate and to others who are firmly determined to meditate.

There are two aspects to the work taking place in or related to meditation:

- One depends on God's presence in a person who gradually surrenders to God, to the divine influence.
- Another presupposes the formation and growth of a new way of feeling (about oneself and others), of responding, which represents a person's new character. We might call this "natural" work to differentiate it from God's direct work.

However, they go together. There cannot be surrender to God and his influence in life if increasingly deeper levels of oneself are not opened up. It is essential to remember that surrender to God is a gradual process and total surrender cannot happen at the start.

That fundamental element of work, *grace,* God's presence in the consciousness and the person, is *invisible* and *indescribable,* and this is a hard blow for immature people who want *to see* and *relate* everything. Such people will not be able to withstand a task in which they do not see or feel their own divinization. Moreover, the work one does toward self-modification and natural restructuring involves conscious and subconscious *levels*. Serious work begins at the subconscious level where authentic changes take place. This is another hard blow for impatient people, for whom saying and doing are the same and for whom planning objectives and reaching them must happen immediately. Here again one needs the beatitude of *those who believed without seeing,* with this difference—that it is not only a matter of faith in God, but also of faith in oneself.

The stages in this work do not stem from one's fancy, but from a person's conditions: from one's work and faithfulness. They are marked by a series of events, symptoms which begin to occur:

- some during daily meditation;
- others in life and the style it adopts.

I will refer to these two aspects, pointing out the stages through which one normally goes. However, before I do that, let me stress that such a classification by stages has its flaws since in reality there are blendings, superpositions, regression and progress; besides there are different rhythms of work for the simple reason that we are dealing with persons and not with chemical elements.

Degrees of Depth in Meditation

Meditation is a continuous process of possessing the object of the meditation, a continuous process of unification of the meditator and the object. This does not happen if a person does not *empty himself,* surrendering to the *direct* experience, without distorting the object of meditation. Consequently the various stages of daily meditation are stages of inner *emptying* and *silencing*.

At the level of character we are *what we think,* but though there is not a perfect contradiction, we can say that at the level of *divinization,* we are *what we keep quiet.*

Thus, I want to present very briefly the degrees of a person's silencing. The extent of this work coincides with a person's facets:

- *Body:* It regains its proper form by means of a progressively deeper relaxation ranging from the most insignificant signs to very intense degrees.

- *Affectivity:* The way of feeling influenced by stimuli upon which a person depends less and less, creating his own stimulation perfectly controlled and oriented in the desired direction.
- *Mind:* There emerges a new consciousness, in comparison with which the previous consciousness is ignorance.

From the various modifications taking place in the person a progressive *disconnection* from the environment occurs during meditation. Later, with the change of consciousness, this disconnection will be a new form of connection, never an absence.

1. First Level

In his book *The Basis of Yoga* Rammurti Mishra calls it *the stage of physical changes,* still very superficial although one may feel it with much depth.

- Physically, the voluntary muscles are affected. *Superficial* relaxation occurs. There is gradual closing of the eyes, anesthesia of the lower legs and of the feet and also of the lower arms and the hands, making it somewhat difficult to raise or move arms and legs.
- Affectively speaking, superficial and temporary pacification takes place. It is partly connected with the lowering of muscular tension.
- At the mental level, one maintains consciousness of the environment. The meditator is aware of what is going on around him.

The following quotation illustrates some of the characteristics corresponding to the beginning of the practice of meditation:

> I did not notice I was breathing. There came a moment so intense that I did not know if I was sitting or in the air, if I had arms and legs. Before such an occurrence and whenever it happens, I have the impression of being asleep.
>
> (*Prayer diary of a nun*)

2. Second Level

The meditator begins to feel a more profound modification of the different parts: body, affectivity and consciousness.

- The body and the senses go more deeply into relaxation and into the withdrawal from the objects of each of the senses.
- All physical sensations, profound and superficial, disappear. Peace increases with a feeling of well-being and calm.

• The mind is enlightened and consciousness expands, growing and filling the person. The person feels he is that consciousness.

Even at this level some degree of connection with the environment is preserved because the senses are not completely absent. They still receive some external stimuli as the following example shows:

> I was completely relaxed and I entered quickly into my meditation. While deeply concentrating, in the midst of a great light, I seemed to be surrounded-submerged-protected by God. I thought I was already tasting what must be the definitive heaven, and mentally, spontaneously, I repeated another word, "Father." I must have said it two or three times, when suddenly I felt immersed in a great light remaining still, with the word in suspense. I was no longer saying anything, but I was simply gazing-loving-adoring. In the course of that meditation, I had another experience, perhaps thirty minutes later, when I heard a woman and a little girl praying softly behind me. Without ceasing to repeat the phrase, still absorbed in that gaze . . . I made these people's wishes mine.
>
> (*Prayer diary of a nun*)

3. Third Level
The Oriental calls this third stage *samadhi* or enlightenment.

• The body is profoundly asleep. There is total anesthesia. The body could undergo an operation without pain. St. John of the Cross also notices it:

Even normally painful things are not felt.[105]
This characteristic stems from the special state of consciousness.

• The consciousness is engrossed in the object of meditation and the surrounding world disappears.

This oblivion of the memory and the paralysis of the imagination are so great at times because the memory is in union with God; that time goes by unnoticed and one does not know what one did during that time. [106]

At this blessed moment everything is transformed: body, affectivity, consciousness. We have a new person, or perhaps the only per-

son who is, or must be. Sivananda alludes to this moment when he
describes the following symptoms:

> During meditation you have no concept of time; no sound, no
> idea of what surrounds you, reaches you. You forget your
> own name and your relationships with others. You enjoy per-
> fect peace and happiness.[107]

This is obviously not the end. It comes later. What Sivananda describes coincides with what I have just quoted from St. John of the
Cross who also warns it can be incorrect:

> Therefore it contains many flaws in its use and external appli-
> cation.[108]

Sivananda also points this out:

> You forget your name and your relationships with others.[109]

However, this happens *at the beginning when union is beginning.* It
helps to identify that phase or moment of inner development. In de-
scribing the same situation with the same symptoms, Sivananda says:
"Little by little, you reach samadhi (union)."
I am not going to specify the different degrees of union, of consciousness or of the impact of grace. I simply want to point to the key
phases of what can be considered active work.

Stages in the Change of Character Through Meditation

Meditation changes a person in the two directions mentioned at
the beginning: the natural aspect—one's character—and the supernatural aspect—God. The divine is only perceived in its reflections, through
the changes it introduces in one's character and life-style. Consequently, I am going to refer in detail to this life-style understood as:

- a more positive way to feel, to experience life;
- a more positive way to feel, to experience life with others;
- a more positive and a more harmonious behavior.

Such traits represent a character in depth. These traits serve to
shape an attitude, to fashion one's attitude. If that attitude is general-

ized so as to influence a person's entire life, we call it "character." So, character is a generalized attitude.

In meditating, one's character, one's attitude are transformed. This happens in stages depending upon the depth reached in regular and continuous meditation—stages signaling the influence of meditation in daily life on one's transformation and one's way of relating to others. All of this goes far beyond the specific time dedicated to meditation, or, rather, meditation expands beyond its own specific time. At first, all that can take place occurs during the brief period of daily meditation, but as one progresses in the practice, something becomes *independent* and manifests itself in its *autonomy* after meditation itself, throughout the day. It indicates a more definitive and profound change. Eventually it becomes permanent, a new way to live, feel and respond, at which point there will be a new character. There are two stages in the formation of this new character. Keep in mind what I said before in regard to stages: they need not form a continuous line without regressions or ups and downs. Fluctuations are in fact the norm until everything becomes *totally normal.*

1. STAGE OF THE INITIAL IMPACT

Most people whom I have met enjoy the initial work. They like the practices which bring them new and refreshing feelings with immediate results of peace and some degree of tranquillity. This really shows how destitute we are since we lack even this basic peace which is only the consequence of better physiological functioning—still superficial—that relaxation and better breathing bring about. The initial lessening of muscular tension and the regulation of breathing produce surprising calm which *attracts* as a toy attracts a child.

This phase is necessarily brief, giving way to routine. People begin to want more than mere peace. The consciousness that nothing is happening begins to take shape and tends to dominate. Many give up after the first stage—superficial people deep down, though it may sound paradoxical, who at times, smugly believing they understand the nature of this work, declare it *to be useless,* or they use the classic rationalization: "There are others ways to work."

2. STAGE OF THE CHANGE IN DEPTH

I have prayer diaries in which people repeat: "Nothing is happening." The phrase points to this stage when people have an overwhelming feeling of *inefficacy:* nothing is taking place. Naturally this impression normally goes with an inner state of dejection and a desire to drop everything. One neither enjoys the *pleasant* feelings of the beginning nor sees the end results. Yet, this stage marks the beginning of

one's transformation. Actually, it all starts at the very first moment of
meditation, but it is not noticed at first.

(a) Assimilation period

This is one of the key characteristics of this moment. When novelty vanishes, one faces what some have called "bricks" or a "wall." One
does not see progress, and yet obscurely an impact exists similar to the
drop of water falling on a rock for the first time.

One is vaguely conscious of the *need* to go through this obviously
unpleasant but necessary stage. This is a period of assimilation, a sort
of underground work occurring below the surface, and this explains
why there is no clear consciousness of what is taking place.

The ascetic master, Sivananda, whom I have often mentioned,
speaks of that moment:

> At first progress will resemble that of a frog, neither steadfast
> nor continuous. You will imagine you have reached the objec-
> tive, and for about fifteen to twenty days you will only expe-
> rience disappointment. You will be leaping from one spot to
> another but not in a continuous development.[110]

Rammurti Mishra also declares:

> Progress will be very slow at first. For the first few days and
> occasionally the first months, you may feel nothing. Howev-
> er, continue with your daily practice, regularly.[111]

This seemingly ungratifying beginning is also mentioned by
Christian mystics:

> As I began to say, one must realize that usually at the begin-
> ning one does not experience this love, but one feels only dry
> and empty.[112]

Differently and on another occasion St. John of the Cross refers to
the same idea, though the formulation differs from that of the Oriental
mystic who does not have the concept of Christian revelation:

> It is true that at the beginning of this new situation, one hard-
> ly notices this loving knowledge.[113]

Many more declarations could be given along with the testimony
of people whom I have seen initiate the way to transformation and

sanctification. This initial period of assimilation is quite natural since we are dealing with changing a person's profound attitude. At the cerebral level, every attitude means a particular brain structure; to change that structure is a matter of time, as Sivananda explains:

At first, new channels and passages are being opened in the mind and the brain.[114]

Apart from this reason true for everyone, there are very specific reasons determined by the specific way of being of all the different people who risk the meditation adventure. We presume they are sincere and moved by an authentic longing for transformation. Yet, even granting this assumption, development will vary from person to person.

St. John of the Cross justifies this period of assimilation in this way:

This burning love is not experienced at first because it has not yet taken hold of the soul due to the impurity of nature or because it has not yet provided a peaceful place within.[115]

This period of pacification and initial purification is absolutely indispensable, and subconsciously it is the only way guaranteeing depth and stability. Unless there is some degree of purification and quieting, people will not be able to progress.

The initial differences vary with each person. The following diagram illustrates something extremely important that people must know if they are to remain steadfast in their work. The psyche or a person's inner state can be compared to a field with ruts:

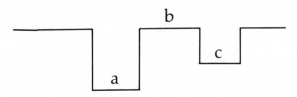

There is unevenness in everyone. When one's attitude is one of sincerity and surrender, work starts at the very beginning and so do the results. If a person is at level "A" and puts a brick to fill in the hole, he will not notice anything. The person at level "B" will immediately notice the *effects* of his work. When "A" reaches ground level, "B" will, of course, be considerably higher. Both have worked. The work of filling in the holes was indispensable, and it demands more patience because one sees nothing. Those who believe they do nothing can be assured that what happens is simply that *they do not see* they are working. In any case, do not make the mistake of thinking that first one must exclusively remove obstacles and then later spiritually shape the inner man. This clarification should make up for what is deficient in the diagram. Purification of inferior nature and the descent or manifestation of superior nature occur simultaneously, and they never happen at first: time and patience are necessary.

The above should suffice to clarify an unpleasant experience which makes perfect sense in the work at hand. It will only happen when one works in depth, which is when the meditator's subconscious is at stake and is deeply affected.

(b) Anxiety connected with growth

Anxiety is not abnormal in itself. As pain, it is a sign. When it goes beyond the possibility of being controlled and used, as an indication of an anomaly which must be corrected, then it is bad.

One of the many causes of anxiety is the *vacuum*. Our normal lives are bound to things and this has two fundamental consequences:

- We receive our security from things or situations, etc.
- We draw our own identity from things. Unfortunately, *we know what we are* through what we have or what we do.

The following pictures illustrate this situation. The center is the person building his own world, peripheral points, in order to be conscious of the center.

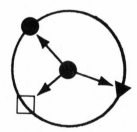

As the person strips himself, freeing himself from all these supports and false mirrors which reflect an erroneous image, the person finds himself as an isolated point.

From this new situation of isolation is born the feeling of isolation and of *insecurity,* anxiety.

This phenomenon occurs in meditation because it is a liberation from everything; the previously normal *limits* are shattered, hence the emergence of anxiety:

- of going beyond the *normal* limits of things which provided security;
- of the automatic destruction of one's *identity* which begins to occur.

This, I repeat, is very common and I have encountered it frequently. As I mentioned before, this underground work is undetected at the conscious level where one experiences darkness and a sense of loss.

The following testimony of a person dedicated to personal transformation through meditation could not prove my point better:

I realize that, before, I enjoyed myself in discotheques, or some other escapes or drinking rum and coke. This no longer suits me. I prefer the peace with which meditation leaves me, but to tell the truth, oftentimes I wonder where this will lead me. More and more I am left without what I was before. When I realized that, not knowing where I was going, reeling in midair not knowing where I might fall, I stopped doing it before Christmas. I escaped again, drinking rum and coke, to convince myself that this busy life was the authentic life. I was telling myself that at least I knew it. So much peace at times! Hell, it frightens me. I can say all this now because I meditate once again. In going back to my former ways, I was trying to enter into this known busy world at all costs. When I think that all this world is slipping away from me and I ignore to what world I am going, I am afraid. On one hand at times I prefer the world I know; on the other hand, if I have days like the past few days since I meditate again, I notice an inner change, more peace, love for everyone, a yearning for life almost without inner or outer ups and downs.

This is a beautiful example of the initial resistance, characteristic of the assimilation period when people seek *reassurance* and guarantees. At first, it is certainly taxing to break the limits one has built for one's own security. Few people take this step. We all desperately seek security, and when at times we try to change mentally, we want to achieve this without risks, in a calculated way, within perfectly known limits. Here the warning of St. John of the Cross is useful: *If you want to go somewhere you do not know, you must go along a way you do not know.* Another person was referring to this moment when she was writing in her prayer diary:

> I seem to be climbing a mountain alone without knowing the way, and besides with this characteristic: I find it increasingly more and more strange and risky.

After having overcome the assimilation period, this person is entering into the phase of enviable transformation vis-à-vis God, self and others. It must be noticed that this person is ready to risk everything. Once again, it is true that *the kingdom of heaven belongs to courageous people.* At that point people seem lost, although

> they have really lost their way, but not as they imagine. What they have lost is the way through their own senses and their first way of feeling, and that is not losing but gaining in the spirituality which is given to them.[116]

3. STAGE OF GREATER INTEGRATION AND MENTAL STABILITY

In the third stage we include all that follows the assimilation period. It is naturally imprecise which presents no difficulty as long as we remain open and available and we have someone to guide us adequately. This guidance is indispensable and so I am not insisting on this phase. I will simply point out some of its characteristics which can be used as orientation in the work. In that phase the work itself serves as an incentive. One observes that everything *is gaining in spirituality.* This stage is one of profound inner unification.

Signs of Progress in the Second Stage

This being a stage wherein one abandons something and begins to gain something, it is essentially "ambiguous," as a religious pointed out in her prayer diary: " . . . and now neither things, nor God completely," referring to their respective attraction. The ambiguity of the signs confuses; one has no reasons to interpret the *new* things which are happening positively, since at times they appear to be bad, and at other times one faintly sees something new and great, but nothing is decisively and clearly perceived. With this background, I am now indicating situations which, either in themselves or in their meanings, are positive and the direct product of meditation. Here are some signs:

1. At times, people experience, as in flashes, something new within, as the following statements express:

> Meditation, however badly I fare in it as *I believe and say*, is helping me discover myself and see what is in the way.

> I notice something new and refreshing within me which I cannot define.

2. Fluctuations are the norm in this phase. Now one feels well, even very well, euphoric; now one is dejected. As Sivananda says, the course is neither continuous nor straight, but it resembles a frog's leaps. Some meditators put it this way:

> Father, why these ups and downs? Sometimes easy, other times so bad?

> I repeated the mantra with peace and serenity. At the end (after an hour) I felt tired and stopped. Could it be due to so much repetition? Other times I did not want to stop. What is happening in the first case? Those days seem of brick, with concrete. I am not complaining. If it must be so, I am satisfied as long as I am not deceiving myself.

> I must tell you that this month . . . has been pretty bad as I see it. Perhaps what I call bad is good because I have seen no joy nor a light announcing: Dawn is coming. Mere routine, repeating without change and every day the same. I have even asked myself "Is this praying?" as if the former ways were better.

> Do I really want to work seriously or not? Am I trying to deceive myself? Is it as we say six one way and half a dozen the other?

> I prayed for over an hour, repeating the mantra and relaxed. I am as of stone. . . . Am I regressing? I think I do what I can, but I felt like a statue in front of a wall.

3. A new peace, not felt before, is beginning to appear. People who meditate constantly declare that they enjoy more peace, serenity, tranquility which some see as *indifference, apathy.*

At night, I prayed a little and stayed awake. I was enjoying great peace.

Over an hour ago, gently, but quickly, I was able to really relax. . . . Immediately great peace, serenity, well-being invaded me.

At first, peace only stays during meditation, but gradually it passes on into daily life and remains throughout the day.

4. One becomes freer from people's opinions. What people may say affects one less. This does not signify contempt of others, but simply that one is more independent, more autonomous.

Consult the chapter on the effects of meditation for examples corresponding to this and the following points.

5. In meditation or because of it, liberation from inner states begins to occur. One sees oneself apart from the fluctuations, even if they occur. One notices something or someone different from one's states of mind which begins to appear as something impersonal. In this phase meditators see all of that as someone looking at rain from behind a window. They begin to feel free from themselves, from the egocentric structure which they had been building over the years.

6. On the other hand, other people seem closer, more loved. Refer to the examples in the aforesaid chapter. Distinctions between people tend to decrease as everyone is becoming interesting and important.

7. Values and what we call *value systems* change. An interview with a meditator began precisely with: "I must tell you that I am convinced I must change my value system." This is normal just as when one notices the need to change clothes or things or ideas because one has outgrown them.

We need not be afraid if at times the change is sudden and seemingly negative. Many people have been told *they were strange.* This is part of the intermediary phase and it will disappear. Let people say what they will. Our own consciousness is a witness of the peace, quietude and personal identity which we are regaining and which people not involved in this *recovery* and *realization* do not comprehend.

The most decisive characteristics are those referring to the way one experiences oneself mentioned in the chapter on effects of meditation.

Signs of Progress in the Third Stage

This is a very rich and varied stage encompassing a vast range of states and personal situations in relation with God and with the world. It is so vast that I do not pretend to explain it. One of the characteristics is a *greater stabilization* of the previous effects. Moreover, people *already notice* some inner plenitude.

I am not dealing with *grace,* God's influx, *out of reach,* and simply limiting myself to the subsequent changes of character which are noticeable and permanent at this stage. In-depth penetration and stability are the traits pointing to the mental integration obtained.

I propose some signs as Blay summarizes them in his book *Creative Personality:*

1. Usually one retains the consciousness of oneself, a positive, pleasant and constructive consciousness. This inner state does not depend upon the fluctuations caused by the changing life circumstances.

2. One's attitude toward people is also positive. One's relationship with others is not determined by what they think of us, nor by their behavior toward us.

3. From this independence stems a *fighting* strength. Let no one think that the person who meditates searching for interiority, is a model of goodness bordering on naiveté. Virtue does not produce fools. This fighting drive or the capacity for struggle and effort is good. Only *aggressiveness* is excluded, for though it resembles this fighting drive, it has nothing in common with it. It stems from a different level, showing a different development, and it tends to very different aims. This fighting spirit is a constructive sign at this stage; whereas aggressiveness tends directly to destroy the foe.

4. Serenity, result of the inner harmony taking place, is constant. I am quoting a fragment of a prayer diary referring to this aspect. There are many more:

Yes, during the day I notice that events affect me differently, though I do not see clearly what it is. It seems that *I cannot get angry;* this phrase perhaps expresses everything.... When things do not go as I want, I find it easier to remain serene.

A person with inner serenity experiences the same external turmoil as everyone else, but he lives more *quietly,* more centered. Living free and detached from things, he can remain in quietude while everything spins around him. For that very reason, a person who meditates, penetrating within himself, becomes less dizzy and tires less. Deep within there is more silence, less frenzy.

5. Life begins to have meaning even in its most minute details.

I notice an inner change, peace, love for everyone, a yearning to live.

I was rushing to love the whole world, knowing that each human being contains a mystery.

6. One of the great signs is a profound religious sense. God becomes closer and more real. As an effect of meditation it appears in that chapter, but I am mentioning it here as the sign of good work. Independently of one's religious context, something appears which is deep within everyone, the world of causes and motivations which directs life and is at the origin of it. One's explanations, ideas, syllogisms and speculations will always be a distortion of *the greatest depth* we have and are. Thus, when one progresses in one's silencing—which occurs in meditation—this inner depth begins to appear. One only gets there when one keeps silent, when one ceases to philosophize to give way to true philosophy that is *wisdom* which is more than a product of logic and conceptualization. At the end of the chapter are some examples of this feeling close to God. Without arguing about their value, let me say that such closeness stems from a psychically desirable state, filled with peace and harmony with very beneficial effects since it stimulates the person, encourages him and projects him toward the world. We cannot expect more in this world in which God manifests himself in signs and inner states. I am perfectly aware that in this life God will only *be seen in darkness,* since *no one has ever seen God.* One guarantee of God's presence can be precisely the *harmony* and peace of someone feeling him to be close.

7. From this greater closeness to God comes a sign which I have verified on various occasions and which St. John of the Cross also points out: the feeling of going backward; to see oneself worse than one thought; to discover evil in oneself which was accepted or ignored before. One begins to perceive a whole world which must be purified and straightened, but it all happens in peace. As the need to get closer to God becomes more urgent, so does the need for purification. Here we have a small vicious circle which is basically virtuous: the more one finds oneself, the more one finds God and vice versa. To find oneself means to rid oneself of the masks and the pretenses, enabling us to consider ourselves alive whereas we are dead. Later, when we find

God, things happen the other way around: we seem to be dead, but we are alive.

To conclude what I have said about the signs of being on the right track, I present the following quotations related to general unspecified aspects, to the global effects of a good meditation:

> If you are in good health, happy, joyful and strong physically and mentally, if your spirit enjoys calm and peace, if you find happiness in your meditation and if your will power increases, know that you are on the right track.[117]

> If you notice satisfaction, optimism, patience, mental pacification; if your voice becomes softer and your body lighter; if you know neither fears nor desires and you lose the taste for things of this world, think that you are progressing on your spiritual course and that you are getting closer to God.[118]

St. John of the Cross gives a summary in *Points of Love:*

> If your soul is more patient in suffering and more tolerant in the lack of desires, it is a sign that it is progressing in virtue.[119]

Though I have not directly referred to prayer which belongs to another dimension, whoever reaches this point in religious meditation has also reached the dimension of prayer. Meditation and prayer merge; their symptoms are now the same. The author of a little book, wisely written, *The Way of a Pilgrim,* refers to the symptoms of prayer. It is a classic work of Oriental spirituality. It deals with the effects and the signs of authentic *inner prayer,* coinciding now with meditation:

> All these experiences taught me that inner prayer produces abundant fruit: sincere love of God, inner peace, rapture of the spirit, purity of thought, agility and strength of the limbs, general well-being, insensitivity to diseases and pains, renewed reasoning energy, fresh understanding of Holy Scripture, understanding the language of every creature, rejection of all vanity, a new insight into sanctity and inner life, and, finally, the great consciousness that God is present and that his love embraces everything.[120]

9

WHY SOME DO NOT PROGRESS IN MEDITATION

- *They Do Not Seek Inner Purification*
- *They Do Not Meditate Regularly*
- *They Lack Determination*
- *Some Erroneous Attitudes in Meditation*

They do not Seek Inner Purification

Some people do not see their progress; we are not dealing with those, since, deep down, they may be progressing. We are dealing with people who do not see their progress because they are not progressing. In my wanderings in this simple and fundamental work of teaching meditation to people, I have encountered both types.

Some do not progress because they simply do not meditate. Some people cannot enter into meditation because they are overburdened and their inner levels are too uneven:

- They are non-integrated, not whole or unified people constantly struggling with themselves and their environment. Such a struggle may be seemingly imperceptible but it suffices to form an obstacle to authentic progress.
- These people are, therefore, unbalanced, burdened. When one is inwardly divided, part of oneself always dominates and rules the other parts, and it is usually the emotional aspect. Sensitivity rules instead of consciousness, and then one's reactions are unforeseen and out of proportion.

Such people are unprepared to see what lies beyond, due to what is lacking within. They cannot pursue an invisible course since they ignore the common visible path. Nature does not work properly in them, and neither will grace for lack of sufficient human basis.

Others do not progress because they trust a technique exclusively, forgetting purification. The vision of God is not, nor was it ever, the result of a technique but the goal of gradual purification. To see God is the beatitude of those whose hearts are pure.

We are not machines, but consciousness which grows or regresses, expresses itself or is inhibited according to how we feel. God's image is within us but oftentimes we obstruct its emergence by our materialistic tendencies, our excessive attachment to things and above all by our excessive ego, as Paul Brunton explains in detail in *The Spiritual Crisis of Man.*

St. John of the Cross expresses the same idea this way:

> We must know that God dwells and remains substantially present in every soul, including the soul of the greatest sinner in the world. . . . Thus, when we speak of union of the soul with God, we are not dealing with this substantial union always existing, but rather of the union of the soul with God which is not continuously activated except when there occurs this likeness issuing from love. . . . And thus, only when the soul rids itself of all that is repugnant and opposed to the divine will, will it be transformed in God by love.[121]

These obstacles are always opposed to love. They represent egocentrism jealously preserved as a privilege. It is very subtle and it destroys the mind and ruins spirituality. Egocentrism also builds its own self-centered spirituality which is not pure since it stems from one's attachments.

Some people are naive and ignorant enough to think that removing the obstacles separating them from the rest of the world, from persons and things, signifies that they will lose their own outlines, their own limits, their personality. We are always falling into this error because we have been taught and we teach the conviction that personality emerges in *opposition* to everything and to everyone.

And so we oppose God because we have shaped a self-centered spirituality which blemishes us and prevents us from seeing any other God than the one we have fabricated and who does not see, speak, hear or understand. Those who fabricate them are not better off since they are nothing more than a projection of their own distorted and weakened consciousness expressing itself.

This lack of purification, these barriers, prevent the clear vision of God, inasmuch as this is possible on earth; they permeate the whole person, affecting all aspects:

- the subconscious, by settling in people's silent but very active layers from which emerge the impulses, motivations and powers influencing the conscious mind;
- the conscious mind, thinking to be autonomous and self-determined whereas it is turned in upon itself and at the service of its own egocentric corruption.

Someone who begins to meditate, uniquely on the strength of a *technique* without sincerely desiring and seeking purification, will be harmed or will not progress because his bad habits or uncontrolled emotions will lead him to distort what he is learning.

In each one of us there is an intermediary factor between the inner and the outer world, the world above and the world below, which we call "consciousness." Its role is to achieve personal integration and the integration with what is above, the divine world, and what is below, the world. If consciousness is impaired or not purified it distorts whatever comes to it and cannot achieve personal integration. This is why St. John of the Cross warns:

So to him who is pure, everything high or low serves for greater good and purity, and in the same way to him who is impure, his very impurity usually leads to evil.[122]

Let no one entertain false hopes about self-*realization* or spiritual transformation if he believes it is the result of magic *formulas*. It only comes from God's grace encountering some channels opened by *discipline* and *purification*. Such is the price which must be paid to be in *another way, to have no ways,* to be a small universe in which we see, as we become purified, that in the final analysis we are *the same,* that everyone and everything is the expression of God. Unless purification takes place at all levels we may lose ourselves in false dreams or end up in utter frustration. We must be ready for total purification including:
1. The body

It must be alert, clean, subject to a functioning rhythm which does not contradict organic laws. Though it has been the way of many saints, the destruction of the body is not the most adequate way to God. To purify the body means to respect the basic laws governing good health and normal functioning.

More directly related to spiritual progress, physical purification signifies the control of corporal appetites. What is specifically most harmful in spiritual progress, completely impairing it, is impurity from the crudest to the most subtle nuances which we appreciate only when we are involved in purification: gluttony, the urge to eat, the uncontrolled action of the senses, wanting to see everything, know everything taste everything, touch everything. The body must be regenerated to allow the influence of the Spirit.

2. The emotions

They must be regenerated for meditation to be beneficial. We must grow to maturity, balance and self-discipline, the practice of virtue to benefit from meditation.

If we approach meditation while nurturing resentment, hidden wounds, pettiness, fears, ill-will, enmity, intolerance, fanaticism, bad temper without acknowledging them and *sincerely* intending to change without losing our peace, we will make no progress in meditation.

3. The mind

Mental purification is also required initially. As the body and emotions are purified, automatically there also occurs a mental purification since the mind is directly influenced by the stimuli from the corporal and affective levels. The emotions greatly condition excessive inner chatter; the appetites struggle to appear, to manifest themselves in the mind, influencing thinking which becomes tense, continuous and at times obsessive, creating doubts, arrogance and all the intellectual vices.

All spiritualities include a period of purification, submission and detachment which is indispensable to penetrate, even *to start* on the way to spiritualization. The Oriental, whose framework we are using, also includes this period made of *yama* and *niyama,* that is: things which must be avoided or negative precepts and things which must be done or positive precepts.

The negative precepts include:

- Non-violence, corresponding to our "You must not kill," not to attempt against life, one's own or others'; to bring *non-violence* to thoughts, words and deeds.
- Not to lie, corresponding to our own similar commandment. Thoughts, words and deeds must be in harmony.
- Not to steal: to destroy the desire to steal.
- Not to do anything against chastity.
- Not to be ambitious: this is the precept of non-ownership.

The positive precepts are:

- Cleanliness, directly referring to the body and the inner organs.
- Contentment: to keep one's mind tranquil and joyful. The classic

definition is: "To abstain from the desire to increase the necessities of existence." To accept disappointments when they come and wherever they come from without complaining, welcoming them calmly.

- Ascesis or physical, verbal and mental austerities. Physical mortifications, calm and suitable speech, inner silence in happiness and concentration.
- Study: self-study. Study of *the sciences related to liberation from existence.*
- Self-abandonment in God.

All these qualities are acknowledged in our own spirituality and in accordance with the Gospel. The Gospel, our way to liberation, also points out the guidelines of purification.

They do not Meditate Regularly

Some think that they can meditate *more or less.* Nothing of importance can be done more or less. We must wholly dedicate ourselves to meditation, and that means with regularity, continuously, daily without exception or variations in the time span. Some meditate twenty minutes one day, one hour the next, then two hours and ten minutes the following day. All spiritual writers insist on regular continuity. Sivananda, for example, says:

It is necessary to meditate regularly. This is an important point, the price of rapid progress and of great success. Even if tangible results are not seen, one needs to continue with sincerity, patience and perseverance. Without a doubt success will come after a while. Do not stop practicing, even for a day or whatever the circumstances may be.[123]

Apart from the fact that there is no progress without regularity, when slumps happen due to days without meditation, the flaws which have not been eliminated but which were beginning to go in second place reappear.

If you are negligent, wavering in your concentration, if your detachment disappears and you cease to practice for a few days out of laziness, adverse forces will lead you away from the true path.[124]

Some people work, skipping along, when here too we realize that nature does not skip along; rather nature looks for succession, continuity. It is in succession and continuity that the wall of self-realization is being settled and constructed. To meditate daily, during the same time and if possible at the same hour, guarantees sure success.

They Lack Determination

A determined person wrote to me:

> It seems that I am not doing much, or, rather, I am not getting much. Do not think that I am discouraged. I will continue if you think I should. I would not want to waste this opportunity *in spite of the cost.*

In the parable of the pearl, the Gospel presents the naive but firm simplicity necessary to those who value the kingdom of God as the only necessity. One must think clearly and be convinced in order to be able to create a determined attitude. St. Teresa refers to this attitude when she writes to her sisters:

> I tell you that it is of the utmost importance to have a great and firm determination not to stop until you reach it (the living water), come what may, whatever may happen, however hard the work may be, whoever may criticize it, whether the goal is reached or not, whether you die on the way and do not have the heart to keep working, or even if the world collapses.[125]

Such is the price one must pay to reach the treasured pearl. One penetrates into the kingdom of God after conquering one's own inner kingdom. Grace builds upon the resolute and open attitude of sustained surrender, and one day the patient and determined searching person will discover the answers within himself. If we persevere in spite of the cost, success will come. St. Teresa corroborates what has been said:

> It is necessary to begin with the assurance that if we do not allow ourselves to be overcome, we will succeed; without any doubt, however little you may gain, you will have a great treasure.[126]

For all of this to happen we must stop complaining and giving in to our frustrations. Many complain about everything, never even helping themselves in their own spiritual evolution. In order to satisfy their consciences they surround themselves by a superficial layer of spirituality which is a totally self-centered structure as was indicated earlier. This structure is useless either to be lifted up or to probe within; it only serves to defend oneself from the anxiety which would inevitably emerge were one conscious of wasting one's time; it serves to protect oneself from God since self-satisfaction produces this seeming spirituality; it destroys the need for personal conversion and the urgent need to respond to God; and finally it means self-defense from the environment since everything satisfying egocentrism signifies *opposition* to others. This may appear exceedingly subtle and it is, but only to those who do not think about it.

The affectivity plays an important role in the lack of determination as it seeks what moves it because of its novelty and the delight it arouses. Determination based only on these factors is not what it seems, as St. John of the Cross points out:

> In fact they are, as we have said, like children who do not move or act under the influence of reason, but under the impulse of pleasure. Such people strive to seek pleasure and spiritual consolation and to that effect they never tire of reading books, going from one meditation to another, in the pursuit of their pleasure even in the things of God. God justly, wisely and lovingly denies it to them, because, otherwise, this gluttony and spiritual greed would lead them to more innumerable evils.[127]

When one is determined to attain self-realization, one is prepared to run physical, emotional and mental risks, all of which are involved in the process of spiritualization. One's capacity to run risks will be the measure of one's determination and therefore of the future degree of success. On the other hand, we must know that success means possessing what is the greatest good—God. He said: "I will be your prize." To this prize St. Paul referred when he wrote: "Run in the same way, meaning to win [it]" (1 Cor. 9:24).

Some Erroneous Attitudes in Meditation

Aside from the great obstacles to meditation, completely ruining it, there are others affecting the moment of meditation itself. I am going to point out a few of those I have encountered in meditators who must constantly rectify attitudes making meditation ineffective.

1. Attitude of those seeking "results"

God is not a result. One must seek God and await his presence. One may easily look for something other than God. A self-centered person imperceptibly falls into the vice of replacing God with something else. One can thus seek strength, depth, new powers without much interest in the source of everything, without seeking the source *for itself* but looking for the benefits coming from arriving at the source. Total, unconditional self-surrender is absolutely indispensable at that moment. Such is the truth of the commandment, "You will have no other God," which in Christian terms is expressed by Paul's solemn profession of faith:

> The life and death of each of us has its influence on others; if we live, we live for the Lord; and if we die, we die for the Lord, so that alive or dead, we belong to the Lord. [128]

This answers the question of those who seek results in meditation or in their relationship with God. The only tempting result is to totally *surrender,* to surrender everything.

2. Impatient attitude

This directly stems from the previous erroneous attitudes when results come slowly. Do not expect anything, as St. John of the Cross says:

> Work without wanting to feel or see anything.[129]

If you expect nothing, you will not despair. Yet some might think that to work, to meditate this way, is meaningless. But the significance of meditation or of any serious work does not come from the expected results but rather from the results achieved, and this point is extremely important.

Impatience is corrected by knowing and accepting the fact that spiritual work is the work of a lifetime. The person who works awaiting results knows that eventually results will happen without being prompted by work and will thus know that meditation justifies itself; it is a result, a gradual in-depth penetration of the mind and a gradual opening to God, and it never ends.

We must cure impatience by expecting nothing while knowing that *we find what we seek in each meditation.* This attitude is authentic and very important. What I want to be, I am becoming in every meditation.

We must believe this in reference to God, because it belongs to the realm of faith. We must also believe it in terms of self because we work with hidden, subconscious levels which will appear one day if they begin to exist in each meditation.

If we work with an attitude oriented to the *present,* knowing we are already obtaining what we are seeking, we will calm ourselves, and the more visible results for which we strive almost exclusively at times appear much before: peace, control, less sensitivity, ability to withstand frustrations, etc.

Whenever we work sincerely, *something* always *happens;* whenever we seek relationship with God we improve though we may not see it. Do not wish *to feel or see anything.*

I now conclude this work undertaken with great love. It is "a way," as some have told me, scornfully implying that it is one of many ways. I simply answer them that it is *an* intelligent way. As for such people it is not a matter of declaring that *there are many ways to go to God,* but a matter of really having a way which leads them to God and to the overcoming of their own *egocentric and sterile spiritual satisfaction.*

Strive to enter by the door leading to life, but this door is a person, Christ, with whom we must establish a personal relationship beyond superficial, emotional and tangible levels. For this in-depth penetration meditation is not *a way;* it is *the way,* man's way, and God will encounter him when he wills, to make us comprehend what is hidden and *to make our hearts burn on the way* as happened to the unbelieving little ones on the way to Emmaus. The encounter with God should be every person's normal encounter if he goes within and probes his life in depth. I wish to conclude modestly with good words for an ending and for reflection: "Let him who has ears, hear." We can still be truly *intelligent.* We must not be satisfied to function always at the same superficial levels where problems are normal and solutions are not normal, or never totally normal. There are other levels, also *normal* within oneself, where solutions are the norm and where problems are only apparently problems. If one meditates, one will see how one's previous ways were a sort of *infancy.* Meditation is an *epiphany,* a manifestation.

Notes

1. Robert Barrat, "La revolución del espíritu," *Gaceta Ilustrada*, No. 951, December 1974, p. 87.
2. *Ibid.*
3. Adelaide Gardner, *Meditazione*, Rome, Astrolabio, 1970, p. 23.
4. *Gaudium et spes*, n. 14.
5. *Ibid.*
6. St. Teresa of Avila, *Camino de perfección*, ch. 24, no. 3, Madrid, BAC, 2nd edition, 1967.
7. Antony Campbell, *Sette stati di conscienzia*, Rome, Astrolabio, 1974, p. 149.
8. Johannes Lotz, *Guida alla meditazione*, Milan, Paoline Ed., 1968, p. 39.
9. Josefina Mainade, *Krishnamurti*, Mexico, Diana, 1972, p. 158.
10. St. John of the Cross, *Noche oscura*, 1, ch. 11, n. 1, Madrid, Apostolado de la Prensa, 8th ed., 1966, p. 425.
11. St. John of the Cross, *Subida al Monte Carmelo*, prologue, n. 3.
12. St. Teresa of Avila, *Camino de perfección*, ch. 21, n. 2.
13. *Ibid.*, ch. 25, n. 2.
14. *Ibid.*, ch. 42, n. 4.
15. Antonio Blay, *Dhyana Yoga*, Barcelona, Cedel, 1965, p. 84.
16. St. John of the Cross, *Subida* . . . II, ch. 12, n. 5.
17. Antonio Blay, *Raja Yoga*, Barcelona, Cedel, 1965, p. 37.
18. Johannes Lotz, *Guida alla meditazione*, Milan, Paoline Ed., 1968, p. 45.
19. Antony Campbell, *Sette stati di conscienza*, Rome, Astrolabio, 1974, p. 139.
20. St. John of the Cross, *Noche oscura*, I, ch. 12, n. 5.
21. St. John of the Cross, *Subida* . . . II, ch. 12, n. 1.
22. *Ibid.*
23. *Ibid.*, II, ch. 12., n. 2.
24. *Ibid.*, II, ch. 4, n. 2.
25. *Ibid.*, III, ch. 2, n. 13.
26. Mircea Eliade, *Le yoga de Patanjali*, quoted by Mariane Kohler, *Técnicas de la serenidad*, Bilbao, El mensajero, 1972, p. 174.
27. Arturo Powell, *El cuerpo mental*, Buenos Aires, Kier, 1965, p. 103.
28. St. John of the Cross, *Subida* . . . II, ch. 12, n. 6.
29. *Ibid.*, ch. 14, n. 4.
30. *Ibid.*, Prologue, n. 7.
31. Paul Chauchard, *El cerebro humano*, Buenos Aires, Paidos, 1958, p. 71.
32. *Ibid.*, p. 74.

33. Arturo Powell, *El cuerpo mental*, Buenos Aires, Kier, 1965, p. 101.

34. Antonio Blay, *La personalidad creadora*, Barcelona, Jims, 1967, p. 320.

35. Swami Akhilananda, *Psicología hindú*. Buenos Aires, Paidos, 2nd ed., 1964, p. 160.

36. Swami Sivananda Sarasvati, *La pratique de la méditation*, Paris, Albin Michel, 1970, p. 95.

37. St. Teresa of Avila, *Camino de perfección*, ch. 40, n. 5.

38. Swami Akhilananda, *Psicología hindú*, p. 147.

39. St. John of the Cross, *Subida* . . . II, ch. 15, n. 1.

40. Angel L. Cilveti, *Introducción a la mística española*, Madrid, Cátedra, 1974, p. 148.

41. *Gaudium et Spes*, n. 18.

42. *Ibid.*, n. 3.

43. *Ibid.*, n. 15.

44. *Ibid.*, n. 22.

45. *Ibid.*, n. 15.

46. Antonio Blay, *Dhyana yoga*, Barcelona, Cedel, 1965, p. 33.

47. Ernesto Wodd, *Curso práctico de concentración mental*, Buenos Aires, Kier, 8th ed., 1972, p. 108.

48. St. John of the Cross, *Subida* . . . II, ch. 13, n. 4.

49. Antonio Blay, *Relajación y energía*, Barcelona, Elicien, 1968, p. 31.

50. Swami Sivananda Sarasvati, *La pratique de la méditation*, Paris, Albin Michel, 1970, p. 256.

51. Arturo Powell, *El cuerpo mental*, Buenos Aires, Kier, 1965, p. 113.

52. St. John of the Cross, *Subida* . . . Prologue, n. 7.

53. *Ibid.*, II, ch. 12, n. 6.

54. Ibid.

55. Antonio Blay, *Dhyana yoga*, Barcelona, Cedel, 1965, p. 75.

56. Swami Sivananda, *La pratique de la méditation*, Paris, Albin Michel, 1970, p. 164.

57. *Ibid.*

58. *Ibid.*

59. St. John of the Cross, *Subida* . . . II, ch. 12, n. 6.

60. *Ibid.*

61. Mouni Sadhu, *Técnica de la concentración*, Buenos Aires, Fabril, 2nd ed., 1971, p. 54.

62. Swami Sivananda, *La pratique de la méditation*, p. 48.

63. St. John of the Cross, *Subida* . . . II, ch. 14, n. 5.

64. Swami Sivananda, *La pratique de la méditation*, p. 120.

65. Antonio Blay, *Dhyana yoga*, p. 80.

66. Swami Sivananda, *La pratique de la méditation*, p. 37.

67. St. John of the Cross, *Subida* . . . II, ch. 15, n. 3.

68. *Ibid.*, II, ch. 15, n. 4.

69. *Ibid.*, III, ch. 4, n. 2.

70. *Ibid.*, II, ch. 15, n. 2.

71. Paul VI, general audience, Dec. 5, 1973, in *Ecclesia* (Dec. 1973), p. 5.
72. Swami Vivekananda, *Raya yoga,* Buenos Aires, Kier, 3rd ed., 1971, p. 107.
73. St. John of the Cross, *Subida* . . . II, ch. 7, n. 8.
74. Johannes Lotz, *Guida alla meditazione,* p. 133.
75. *Ibid.,* p. 134.
76. Swami Sivananda, *La pratique de la méditation,* p. 165.
77. Antonio Blay, *Dhyana yoga,* p. 101.
78. *Ibid.*
79. *Ibid.*
80. *Ibid.,* p. 102.
81. St. Augustine, *Comentarios sobre los salmos,* Ps. 32, sermon 1.
82. Antony Campbell, *Sette stati di conscienza,* p. 49.
83. Mouni Sadhu, *Técnica de la concentración,* p. 200.
84. St. John of the Cross, *Subida* . . . II, ch. 12, n. 5.
85. *Ibid.,* ch. 17, n. 5.
86. *Ibid.,* ch. 4, n. 5.
87. *Ibid.,* ch. 12, n. 6.
88. *Ibid.,* ch. 12, n. 7.
89. *Ibid.,* ch. 12, n. 6.
90. *Ibid.,* ch. 12, n. 8.
91. Swami Akhilananda, *Psicología hindú,* Buenos aires, 1964, p. 142.
92. Swami Sivananda, *Luz, poder y energía,* Buenos Aires, 1971, p. 42.
93. Antonio Blay, *Dhyana yoga,* p. 10.
94. Tsongkhapa, *Lamrin,* quoted by Alexandra David-Neil: *La Connaissance Transcendante,* Paris, Adyar, 1958, p. 28.
95. Antonio Blay, *La personalidad creadota,* Barcelona, Jims, 2nd ed., 1967, p. 130.
96. Antonio Blay, *Relajación y energía,* Barcelona, Elicien, 2nd ed., 1968, p. 111.
97. Antonio Blay, *Dhyana yoga,* p. 34.
98. Fernando González, *Canciones súbitas,* in ABC, Dec. 2, 1974.
99. Philippians 4:7.
100. Mouni Sadhu, *Técnica de la concentración,* Buenos Aires, Fabril, 2nd ed., 1971, p. 223.
101. Swami Vishnudevananda, *El libro de yoga,* Madrid, Alianza Editorial, 1974, p. 323.
102. St. John of the Cross, *Subida* . . . II, ch. 14, n. 11.
103. Swami Sivananda, *La pratique de la méditation,* p. 315.
104. St. John of the Cross, *Subida* . . . III, ch. 3, n. 4.
105. St. John of the Cross, *Subida* . . . III, ch. 2, n. 6.
106. *Ibid.*
107. Swami Sivananda, *La pratique de la méditation,* p. 315.
108. St. John of the Cross, *Subida* . . . III, ch. 2, n. 6.
109. Swami Sivananda, *La pratique de la méditation,* p. 315.

110. *Ibid.,* p. 172.

111. Rammurti Mishra, *Fundamentos de yoga,* Buenos Aires, Dédalo, 1973, p. 38.

112. St. John of the Cross, *Noche oscura,* 1, ch. 11, n. 2.

113. St. John of the Cross, *Subida* . . . II, ch. 13, n. 7.

114. Swami Sivananda, *La pratique de la méditation,* p. 83.

115. St. John of the Cross, *Noche oscura,* I, ch. 11, n. 1.

116. St. John of the Cross, *Subida* . . . II, ch. 14, n. 4.

117. Swami Sivananda, *La pratique de la méditation,* p. 231.

118. *Ibid.,* p. 18.

119. St. John of the Cross, Avisos, *Puntos de Amor,* p. 41.

120. Anonymous, *El peregrino ruso,* Madrid, Espiritualidad, 1974, p. 57.

121. St. John of the Cross, *Subida* . . . II, ch. 5, n. 3.

122. St. John of the Cross, *Subida* . . . III, ch. 26, n. 6.

123. Swami Sivananda, *La pratique de la méditation,* p. 118.

124. *Ibid.,* p. 59.

125. St. Teresa of Avila, *Camino de perfección,* ch. 21, n. 2.

126. *Ibid.,* ch. 35, n. 2.

127. St. John of the Cross, *Noche oscura,* I, ch. 6, n. 6.

128. Romans 14:7–8.

129. St. John of the Cross, *Subida* . . . II, ch. 15, n. 2.